THE COMPLETE
CHILDREN'S
ATLAS

THE COMPLETE
CHILDREN'S
ATLAS

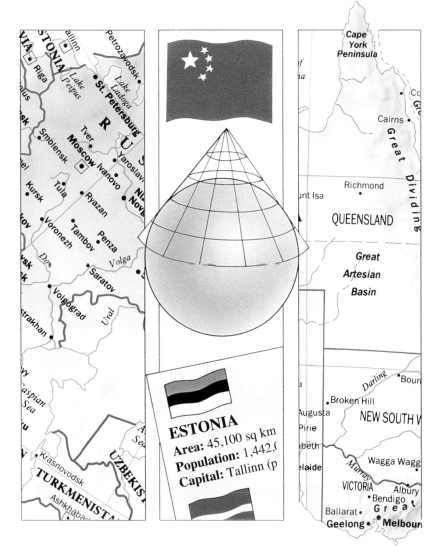

MALCOLM PORTER

CHERRYTREE BOOKS

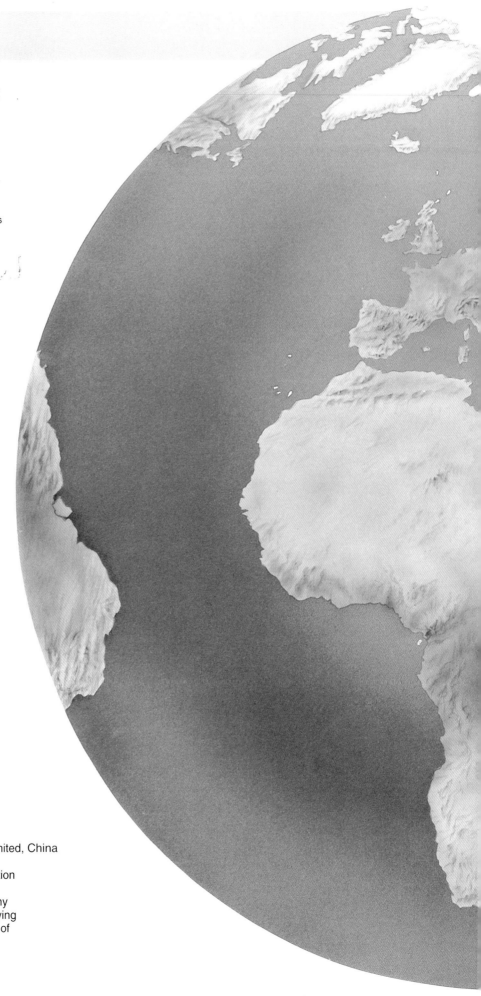

A Cherrytree Book

Designed and produced by
A S Publishing
Consultant editor Keith Lye
Assistant editor Paul Dempsey

This revised and updated edition
published 2007
by Cherrytree Books, part of the
Evans Publishing Group
2A Portman Mansions
Chiltern St
London W1U 6NR

Copyright © Malcolm Porter and A S
Publishing 2007

British Library Cataloguing in Publication
data
Porter, Malcolm
    The complete children's atlas
            1.Children's atlases 2.Atlases,
            British-Juvenile literature
            I.Title
            912
ISBN 1842344358
13 digit ISBN (from 1 January 2007)
97818342344354

Printed by Midas Printing International Limited, China

CONTENTS

Planet Earth

Our Earth is one of the nine planets that circle the Sun. It is the third planet from the Sun. Today, we can see photographs of the Earth taken from space. These show land areas, called continents, and blue seas and oceans.

Maps show the same things, but they give much more information than space photographs. They show the names and positions of cities and towns, and other features such as rivers and mountains.

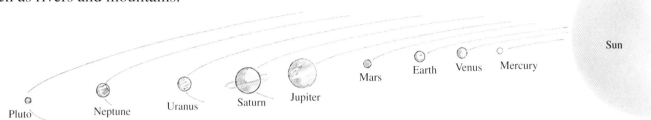

As the Earth circles the Sun, it spins on its axis, an imaginary line joining the North Pole, the centre of the Earth and the South Pole.

Some lines appear on maps. One line around the middle of the Earth, exactly halfway between the North and South Poles, is called the Equator. Other lines are called the Tropic of Cancer in the northern half of the world, and the Tropic of Capricorn in the southern half. Two important lines go round the cold areas near the poles. They are the Arctic and Antarctic Circles.

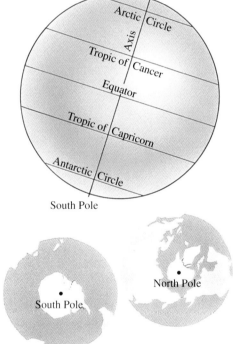

Land areas		
	Area (sq km)	Area (sq miles)	Population
North America	24,249,000	9,363,000	512,422,000
South America	17,835,000	6,886,000	371,271,000
Europe*	6,222,600	2,402,000	585,594,000
Russia	17,075,400	6,593,000	142,420,000
Asia*	31,181,000	12,039,000	3,902,374,000
Africa	30,330,000	11,694,000	891,437,000
Australia and the Pacific	8,508,000	3,285,000	32,744,000
Antarctica	14,000,000	5,400,000	

*Excluding Russia

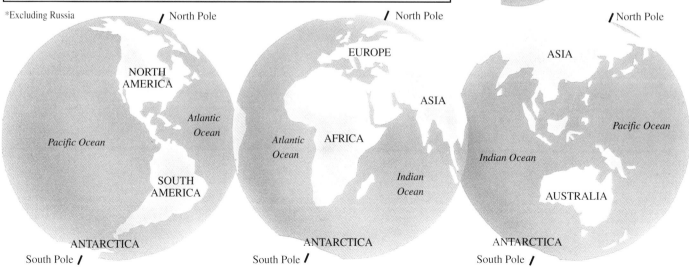

6

World records

Mountains
The highest mountains in five continents are shown on the right. The world's highest peak is Mount Everest.

Aconcagua
(SOUTH AMERICA)
6,959m
(22,831ft)

McKinley
(NORTH AMERICA)
6,194m
(20,320ft)

Everest
(ASIA)
8,848m
(29,028ft)

Kilimanjaro
(AFRICA)
5,895m
(19,340ft)

Elbrus
(EUROPE)
5,633m
(18,481ft)

Rivers
The world's longest rivers are the Nile in Africa and the Amazon in South America.

Darling (AUSTRALIA) 2,739 km (1,702 miles)

Volga (EUROPE) 3,531km (2,194 miles)

Mississippi (NORTH AMERICA) 3,779 km (2,348 miles)

Chang Jiang (ASIA) 5,530 km (3,436 miles)

Amazon (SOUTH AMERICA) 6,448 km (4,007 miles)

Nile (AFRICA) 6,670 km (4,145 miles)

Deserts
Deserts cover about a seventh of the world's land areas. The Sahara in North Africa is the largest.

Sahara (AFRICA) 8,400,000 sq km (3,250,000 sq miles)

Great Australian Desert (AUSTRALIA) 1,550,000 sq km (600,000 sq miles)

Arabian Desert (ASIA) 1,300,000 sq km (500,000 sq miles)

Gobi Desert (ASIA) 1,170,000 sq km (450,000 sq miles)

Kalahari Desert (AFRICA) 520,000 sq km (200,000 sq miles)

Lakes
The world's largest lake is the Caspian Sea, so called because its water is salty. The largest freshwater lake is Lake Superior.

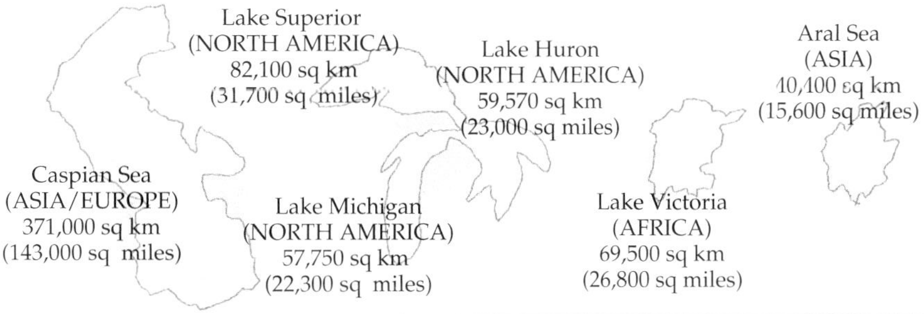

Lake Superior
(NORTH AMERICA)
82,100 sq km
(31,700 sq miles)

Lake Huron
(NORTH AMERICA)
59,570 sq km
(23,000 sq miles)

Aral Sea
(ASIA)
40,100 sq km
(15,600 sq miles)

Caspian Sea
(ASIA/EUROPE)
371,000 sq km
(143,000 sq miles)

Lake Michigan
(NORTH AMERICA)
57,750 sq km
(22,300 sq miles)

Lake Victoria
(AFRICA)
69,500 sq km
(26,800 sq miles)

Islands
Islands are land areas surrounded by water. The world's largest island, Greenland, is mostly covered by ice.

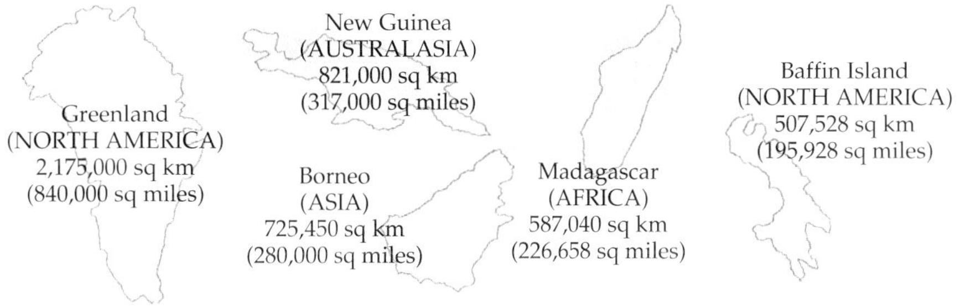

New Guinea
(AUSTRALASIA)
821,000 sq km
(317,000 sq miles)

Baffin Island
(NORTH AMERICA)
507,528 sq km
(195,928 sq miles)

Greenland
(NORTH AMERICA)
2,175,000 sq km
(840,000 sq miles)

Borneo
(ASIA)
725,450 sq km
(280,000 sq miles)

Madagascar
(AFRICA)
587,040 sq km
(226,658 sq miles)

Deeps and depressions
The deepest point on land is the shore of the Dead Sea in Israel and Jordan. The deepest part of the oceans is in the Marianas Trench, in the Pacific.

Lowest point on land
Dead Sea shoreline (ASIA)
400m (1,312ft) below sea level

Deepest point in the oceans
Marianas Trench (PACIFIC OCEAN)
11,034m (36,200ft)

Deepest lake
Lake Baykal (ASIA)
1,940m (6,365ft) deep
or 1,485m (4,872ft) below sea level

Measuring the Earth

Models of the Earth are called globes. The surfaces of globes are marked with networks of lines.

Some lines run round the globe. They are called lines of latitude or parallels. The Equator, the Tropics of Cancer and Capricorn, and the Arctic and Antarctic Circles are all lines of latitude.

Other lines on globes run at right angles to the lines of latitude, through both the North and South Poles. These are lines of longitude, or meridians.

Lines of latitude and longitude are marked on maps, which show the globe, or parts of it, on flat pieces of paper. The position of every place on Earth has its own latitude and longitude.

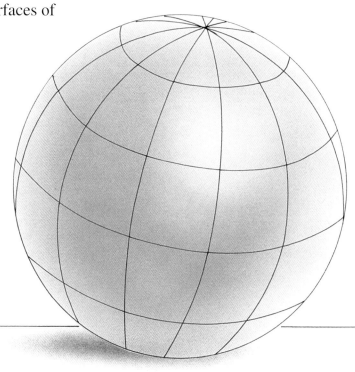

Latitude

The latitude of the Equator, which divides the Earth into two equal halves, called hemispheres, is 0 degrees. The latitude of the North Pole is 90 degrees North (90°N), while the latitude of the South Pole is 90 degrees South (90°S).

The latitude of places between the Equator and the Poles is measured in degrees north or south of the Equator. For example, the latitude of Washington D.C. is nearly 39 degrees North. This means that the angle formed at the centre of the Earth between the Equator and Washington D.C. is nearly 39 degrees.

The Tropic of Cancer is latitude 23$\frac{1}{2}$ degrees North, while the Tropic of Capricorn is 23$\frac{1}{2}$ degrees South. The Arctic Circle is 66$\frac{1}{2}$ degrees North, while the Antarctic Circle is 66$\frac{1}{2}$ degrees South.

Longitude

Lines of longitude are measured 180 degrees east and west of the prime meridian, or 0 degrees longitude. The prime meridian runs through the North Pole, Greenwich, in London, England, and the South Pole. The line was agreed at an international conference in 1884.
Washington D.C., for example, is situated at 77 degrees West. This means that the angle formed at the centre of the Earth between the prime meridian and another line of longitude running through Washington D.C. is 77 degrees west of the prime meridian.

The 180 degree line of longitude east and west of the prime meridian runs through the Pacific Ocean, on the far side of the world from the prime meridian. The prime meridian and the 180 degree line of longitude divide the Earth into two hemispheres, east and west, in the same way that the Equator divides north and south.

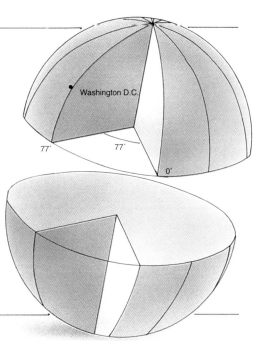

Map projections

One of the problems faced by map-makers is that it is impossible to show the Earth on a flat piece of paper without distorting it to some extent. You can understand the problem if you imagine that the world is an orange. If you peel the orange, there is no way that you can stretch the peel flat without breaking it up and crushing the pieces.

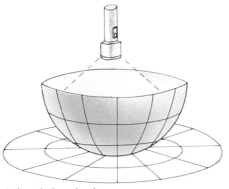

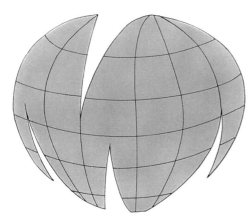

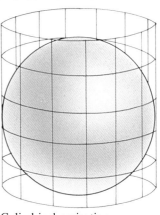

Azimuthal projection

To meet this problem, map-makers use map projections. Imagine a glass globe with the network of lines of latitude and longitude (called graticules) engraved on it. Put a light inside the globe and the graticules will be cast, or projected, on to a flat sheet of paper touching it at one point to produce an *azimuthal projection*. Imagine doing the same with a paper cylinder to produce a *cylindrical projection* or a paper cone to produce a *conical projection*.

Cylindrical projection

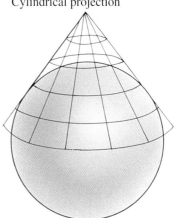

Conical projection

Projections in this atlas

The projections shown above are called perspective projections. But, in practice, map-makers seldom use these projections. Instead, they use projections which they develop using mathematics, so that they can reproduce accurately areas, shapes, distances and directions. Projections used for maps of the world can preserve some of these features, though no single projection can show them all.

The maps that show the continent at the beginning of each chapter of this atlas have been specially drawn to show how the continent looks from space. The map on the right shows how Africa on page 69 would look with lines of latitude and longitude.

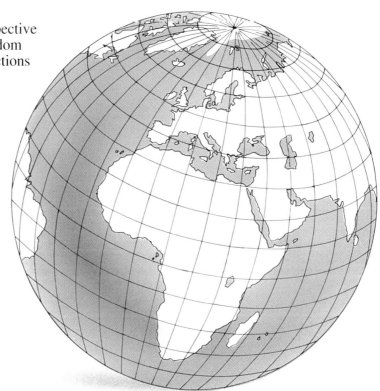

How to Use the Atlas

To put as much information as possible on a map, map-makers use symbols. To get the most out of the maps in this atlas, it helps to know the symbols.

Cities with a population over 1 million people	**New York City** •
Cities with a population between 100,000 and 1 million	**Atlantic City** •
Towns with a population of below 100,000	Vineland •
Capital city	**Washington D.C.** ▣
State capital	★ **Phoenix**
Mountain with its height	△ Mt McKinley 6194m
Mountain range	**Catskill Mts**
Dam	┤
Island	**Island**
Archaeological site	∴

River	*River*
Canal	*Canal*
Lake	*Lake*
Country name	**CANADA**
Province or state name	MARYLAND
Country border	———

Key to land colouring

Forest	
Crops	
Dry Grassland	
Desert	
Tundra	
Polar	

Maps in the Atlas

The atlas starts with views of the world as a whole. The physical map of the world on pages 12-13 shows the world's main land features, while the political map on pages 14-15 shows the countries into which the world is divided.

The atlas contains sections on North America, South America, Europe, Asia, Africa and Australia. Each section has a map showing where the continent is situated on the globe and the countries it contains. Other maps show groups of countries (or states) in the continent.

If you want to know facts about a country, such as its population or area, look at the table alongside the map.

The last section of the atlas has maps of the oceans and the polar regions.

Populations

Many large cities, such as Boston, have metropolitan area populations (2,871,000) that are greater than the city figures (569,000). Such cities have larger dot sizes on the map to emphasize their importance.

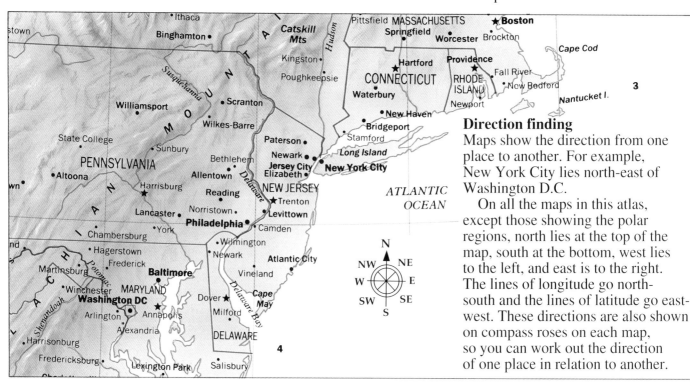

Direction finding

Maps show the direction from one place to another. For example, New York City lies north-east of Washington D.C.

On all the maps in this atlas, except those showing the polar regions, north lies at the top of the map, south at the bottom, west lies to the left, and east is to the right. The lines of longitude go north-south and the lines of latitude go east-west. These directions are also shown on compass roses on each map, so you can work out the direction of one place in relation to another.

Using the index

To find a place in this atlas, use the index at the back of the book.

After each place name you will find a number and then a letter and a number. For example, if you want to find Rome, the capital of Italy, you will find the following entry in the index:

Rome 52 B3

You should then turn to page 52, where you will find the map of Italy and South-Eastern Europe. Look for the square on the map labelled B at the top and 3 on the left-hand side. You will then find Rome in that square.

Scales and distance

Maps are drawn to scale.This means that you can find the distance between places on a map.

The maps in this atlas have a scale line marked in kilometres and miles. Place a piece of paper on this line and mark off the distances shown. If you want to know the distance from San Diego to Lake Havasu City, place your piece of paper on the map with the zero end on San Diego. You will find that the distance to Lake Havasu City is about 300 kilometres (200 miles). See if you can find the distance between Cedar City and Flagstaff.

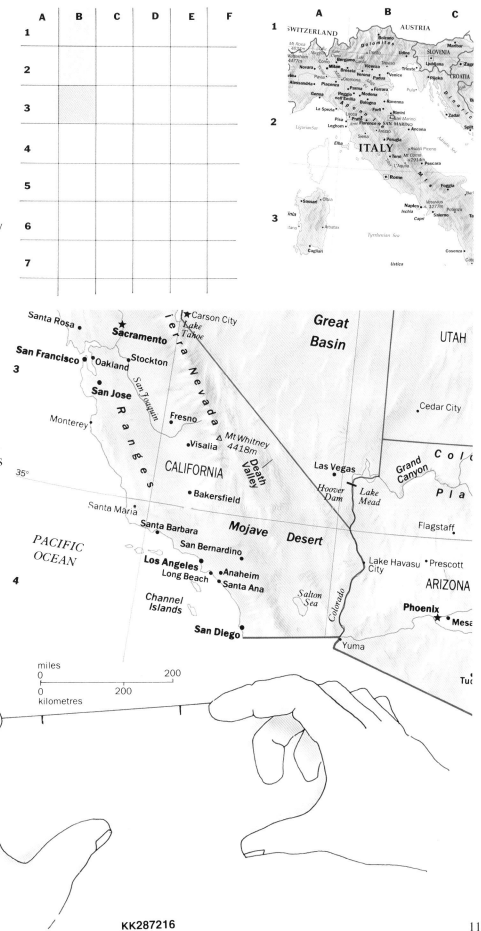

The Physical World

ARCTIC OCEAN

Baffin Island

Greenland

Arctic Circle

Mt McKinley

Hudson Bay

R o c k y   M t s

Great Plains

Great Lakes

NORTH AMERICA

Appalachian Mts

Mississippi

Tropic of Cancer

Gulf of Mexico

West Indies

Caribbean Sea

ATLANTIC OCEAN

Equator

Amazon

A n d e s   M t s

Selvas

Atacama Desert

PACIFIC   OCEAN

SOUTH AMERICA

Tropic of Capricorn

Aconcagua

Tasman Sea

New Zealand

Patagonia

Antarctic Circle

ANTARCTICA

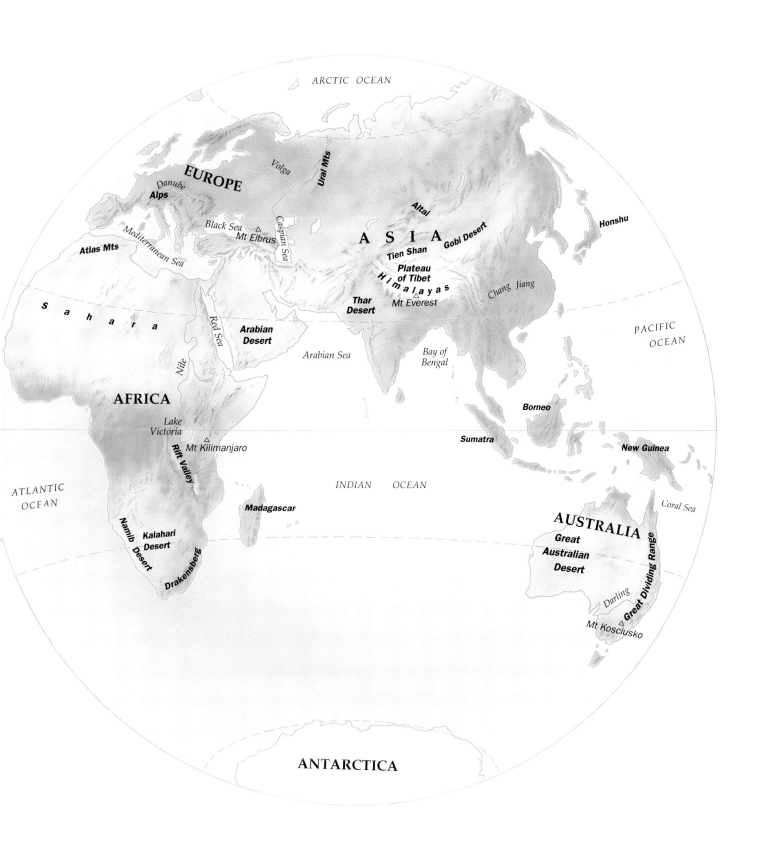

ARCTIC OCEAN

Volga

EUROPE

Danube

Alps

Ural Mts

Altai

Honshu

Black Sea

Mediterranean Sea

Mt Elbrus

Caspian Sea

A S I A

Tien Shan

Gobi Desert

Atlas Mts

**Plateau
of Tibet**

H i m a l a y a s

Chang Jiang

S a h a r a

Red Sea

**Thar
Desert**

Mt Everest

**Arabian
Desert**

PACIFIC
OCEAN

Nile

Arabian Sea

*Bay of
Bengal*

AFRICA

Borneo

*Lake
Victoria*

Sumatra

New Guinea

Mt Kilimanjaro

Rift Valley

ATLANTIC
OCEAN

INDIAN   OCEAN

Coral Sea

Madagascar

AUSTRALIA

**Namib
Desert**

**Kalahari
Desert**

**Great
Australian
Desert**

Great Dividing Range

Drakensberg

Darling

Mt Kosciusko

ANTARCTICA

13

The Political World

The world is divided into more than 200 countries. The biggest country is the Russian Federation. The smallest independent country is Vatican City, which covers only 44 hectares (109 acres) in Rome, Italy's capital city.

Most of the world's countries are independent, but some are dependencies – that is, they are ruled by other countries. French Guiana on this map is not an independent country. It is ruled as an overseas region of France.

Most dependencies are tiny island countries. They are so small that they do not appear on this map. The map of the Caribbean on pages 32 and 33 shows several tiny dependencies not shown on this map. They include Montserrat (U.K.), Martinique (France) and the Netherlands Antilles.

GREENLAND

USA

CANADA

UNITED STATES OF AMERICA

MEXICO

BAHAMAS

CUBA

DOMINICAN REPUBLIC

ST. CHRISTOPHER & NEVIS

HAITI

ANTIGUA & BARBUDA

BELIZE

JAMAICA

DOMINICA

GUATEMALA

HONDURAS

ST. LUCIA

EL SALVADOR

NICARAGUA

ST. VINCENT &
GRENADINES

BARBADOS

GRENADA

COSTA RICA

PANAMA

TRINIDAD & TOBAGO

VENEZUELA

GUYANA

SURINAM

FRENCH GUIANA (Fr.)

COLOMBIA

ECUADOR

PERU

BRAZIL

BOLIVIA

PARAGUAY

CHILE

URUGUAY

ARGENTINA

1 ANDORRA
2 MONACO
3 LIECHTENSTEIN
4 SAN MARINO
5 VATICAN CITY
6 SLOVENIA
7 CROATIA
8 SERBIA
9 BOSNIA & HERCEGOVINA
10 ALBANIA
11 MACEDONIA
12 MONTENEGRO

Information panels

This atlas contains panels with information about all the independent countries of the world, including their area, population and capital. Extra details, including information about religions, languages, the economy or main products, and the nature of the government, are given about as many countries as space allows.

Many countries are republics, with a president as head of state. Most republics are democracies, with elected parliaments, though some republics are not democratic.

Other countries are monarchies. Their head of state is a king or queen, though most are actually ruled by elected governments. Some major countries in the Commonwealth, such as Australia, Canada, New Zealand and Britain itself, are constitutional monarchies. They recognize the British queen as their head of state, but in practice democratically elected governments rule these countries.

North America

North America, the third largest continent, contains the world's largest island, Greenland, and three huge countries: Canada, the United States and Mexico. It also includes the smaller countries of Central America and the islands of the Caribbean Sea.

The land of North America includes icy areas in the north and warm tropical places in the south. The United States contain both the Mississippi-Missouri River, North America's longest, and the highest mountain, Mount McKinley in Alaska.

North America contains 23 independent countries. Its total population is about 500 million. Canada and the United States are rich, developed countries. But many people of Central America and the Caribbean are poor.

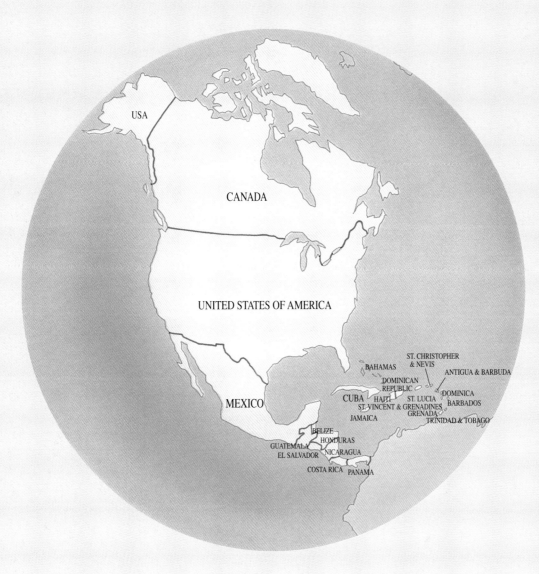

Canada and Greenland

CANADA

Area: 9,976,139 sq km (3,851,809) sq miles); the world's second largest country

Highest point: Mount Logan 6,050m (19,849ft)

Population: 32,805,000

Capital: Ottawa (pop 1,093,000)

Largest cities:
Toronto (4,600,000)
Montreal (3,400,000)

Official languages: English, French

Religion: Christianity (89.2%)

Main products: Motor vehicles and other manufactures, paper, minerals, farm products

Currency: Canadian Dollar

Government: Constitutional monarchy

ST. PIERRE & MIQUELON

Area: 242 sq km (93 sq miles)

Population: 6,300

Capital: St. Pierre

Government: French territory

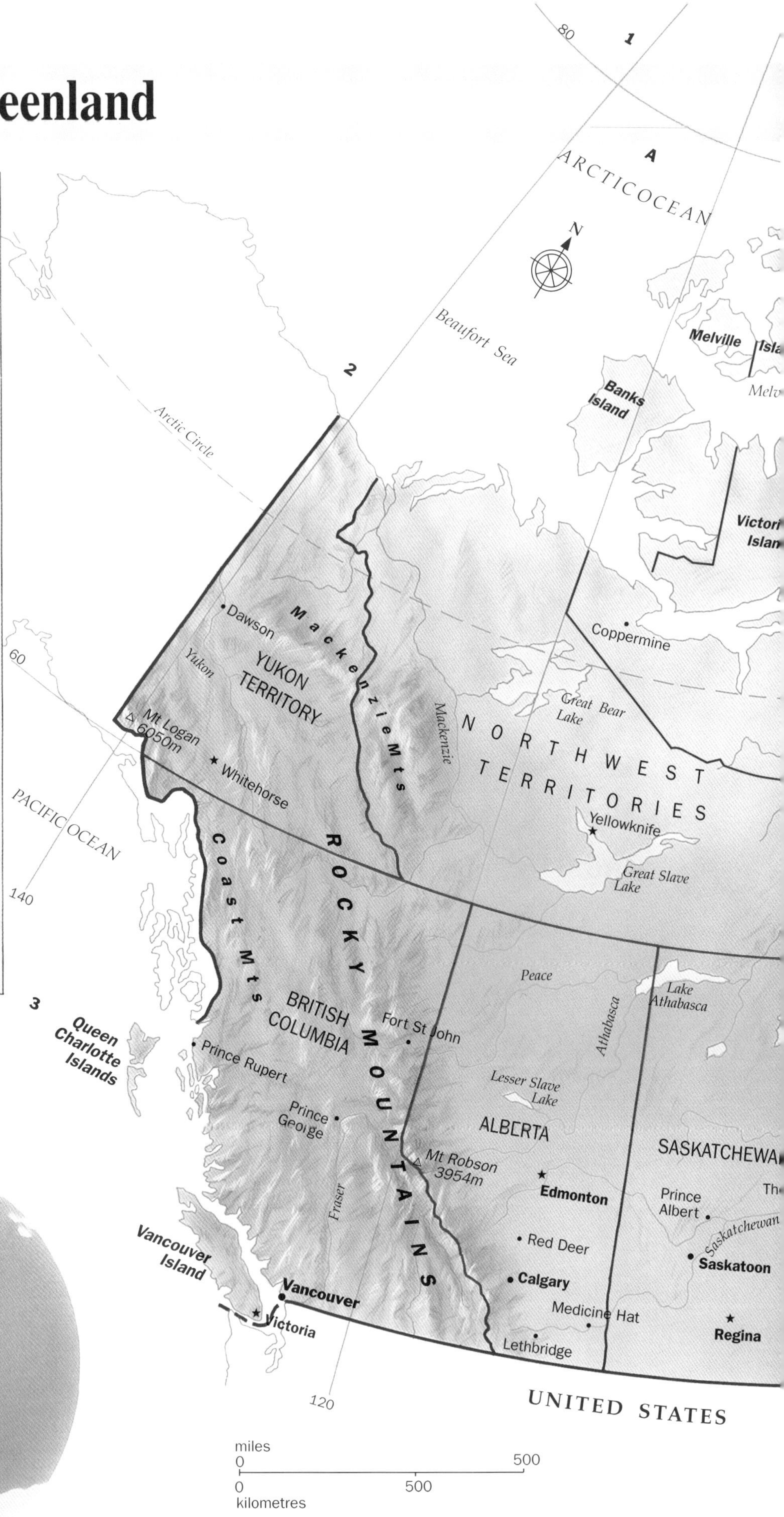

ARCTIC OCEAN

Beaufort Sea

Melville Isla

Banks Island

Melv

Victori Islan

Mackenzie Mts

Dawson

Yukon

YUKON TERRITORY

Coppermine

Great Bear Lake

NORTHWEST

Mt Logan 6050m

Whitehorse

Mackenzie

TERRITORIES

Yellowknife

Great Slave Lake

PACIFIC OCEAN

Coast Mts

ROCKY

BRITISH COLUMBIA

Peace

Lake Athabasca

Queen Charlotte Islands

Prince Rupert

Fort St John

Athabasca

Lesser Slave Lake

ALBERTA

SASKATCHEWA

Prince George

MOUNTAINS

Mt Robson 3954m

Edmonton

Prince Albert

The

Saskatchewan

Fraser

Red Deer

Saskatoon

Vancouver Island

Calgary

Vancouver

Medicine Hat

Victoria

Lethbridge

Regina

UNITED STATES

miles
0   500

0   500
kilometres

Arctic Circle

C   D   E   F

Ellesmere Island

Thule

Gunnbiorn △ 3700m

Baffin Bay

GREENLAND (DENMARK)

Angmagssalik

Devon Island

thurst sland

Somerset Island

rince of Wales sland

Disko Island

Godhavn

Baffin Island

Davis Strait

Godthaab

Frederikshaab

Cape Farewell

40°

King William Island

Melville Peninsula

GREENLAND

Area: 2,175,600 sq km (840,000 sq miles)

Population: 56,000

Capital: Godthaab (pop 13,400)

Government: Self-governing part of Denmark

Iqaluit

Frobisher Bay

Southampton Island

Hudson Strait

NUNAVUT

Ungava Peninsula

Nain

N E W F O U N D L A N D

Eskimo Point

Hudson Bay

Labrador

Churchill

MANITOBA

Churchill

James Bay

Fort Albany

Fort Rupert

Q U E B E C

Anticosti Island

Corner Brook

Newfoundland

St John's ★

St Pierre & Miquelon (FRANCE)

Lake Winnipeg

Chicoutimi

NEW BRUNSWICK

PRINCE EDWARD ISLAND

Glace Bay

ake anitoba

Quebec

Moncton

Charlottetown

Sydney

Winnipeg ★

Kenora

Trois Rivieres

St. Lawrence

NOVA SCOTIA

ndon

Timmins

Montreal

Fredericton ★

Saint John

Halifax

Thunder Bay

O N T A R I O

Ottawa

Hull

Ottawa

Cape Sable

60°

Lake Superior

Sault Ste. Marie

Sudbury

Peterborough

Kingston

A T L A N T I C   O C E A N

Lake Huron

Kitchener

Oshawa

Lake Ontario

Hamilton

London

Toronto

Niagara Falls

Lake Michigan

Windsor

Lake Erie

80°

19

United States of America

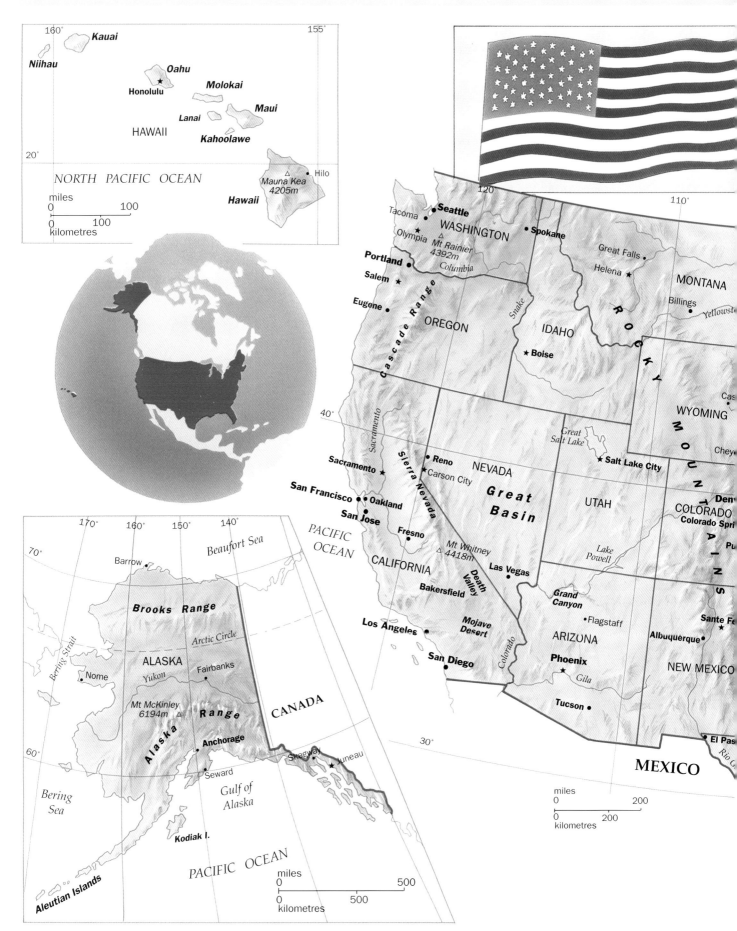

HAWAII

Kauai
Niihau
Oahu
Honolulu
Molokai
Maui
Lanai
Kahoolawe

NORTH PACIFIC OCEAN

miles
0   100

0   100
kilometres

Mauna Kea
4205m
Hilo
Hawaii

ALASKA MAP

Beaufort Sea

PACIFIC OCEAN

Barrow

Brooks Range

Arctic Circle

ALASKA

Yukon
Fairbanks

Nome

Mt McKinley
6194m

Alaska Range

CANADA

Anchorage

Skagway
Juneau
Seward

Bering Strait

Bering Sea

Gulf of Alaska

Kodiak I.

PACIFIC OCEAN

Aleutian Islands

miles
0   500

0   500
kilometres

MAIN MAP

Tacoma
Seattle
WASHINGTON
Spokane
Olympia
Mt Rainier
4392m
Columbia
Portland
Salem
Eugene
Cascade Range
OREGON
Snake
IDAHO
Boise

Great Falls
Helena
MONTANA
Billings
Yellowst
ROCKY

Sacramento
Sacramento
San Francisco
Oakland
San Jose
Fresno
Sierra Nevada
Reno
Carson City
NEVADA
Great Basin
Great Salt Lake
Salt Lake City
UTAH
WYOMING
Cas
Cheye
COLORADO
Den
Colorado Spri

Mt Whitney
4418m
CALIFORNIA
Bakersfield
Los Angeles
San Diego
Las Vegas
Death Valley
Mojave Desert
Lake Powell
Grand Canyon
Flagstaff
ARIZONA
Phoenix
Colorado
Gila
Tucson
Pu
Sante Fe
Albuquerque
NEW MEXICO

MEXICO
El Pas
Rio G

miles
0   200

0   200
kilometres

20

UNITED STATES

Area: 9,529,063 sq km (3,679,192 sq miles); the world's fourth largest country
Highest point: Mount McKinley, Alaska, 6,194m (20,322ft): the highest peak in North America
Population: 295,734,000

Capital: Washington D.C. (pop 553,000)
Largest cities:
New York City (8,104,000)
Los Angeles (3,846,000)
Chicago (2,862,000)
Houston (2,013,000)
Philadelphia (1,470,000)
Official language: English
Religion: Christianity (87.1%)

Economy: *Agriculture:* grains, oil crops, cattle, dairy products; *Mining:* coal, copper, gold, oil, iron, nickel, silver, uranium, zinc; *Industry:* machinery and transport equipment, chemicals, food products
Currency: U.S. Dollar
Government: Federal Republic

USA North-Eastern States

 Kentucky

Area: 104,659 sq km (40,410 sq miles)
Population: 4,146,000
Capital: Frankfort (pop 27,000)
Largest city: Lexington (pop 266,000)

 West Virginia

Area: 62,758 sq km (24,232 sq miles)
Population: 1,815,000
Capital and largest city: Charleston (pop 52,000)

 Virginia

Area: 105,586 sq km (40,767 sq miles)
Population: 7,460,000
Capital: Richmond (pop 192,000)
Largest city: Virginia Beach (pop 440,000)

 Pennsylvania

Area: 119,251 sq km (46,043 sq miles)
Population: 12,406,000
Capital: Harrisburg (pop 47,000)
Largest city: Philadelphia (pop 1,470,000)

 New York

Area: 136,583 sq km (52,735 sq miles)
Population: 19,227,000
Capital: Albany (pop 94,000)
Largest city: New York City (pop 8,104,000) largest in the USA

 Vermont

Area: 24,900 sq km (9,614 sq miles)
Population: 621,000
Capital: Montpelier (pop 8,000)
Largest city: Burlington (pop 39,000)

 New Hampshire

Area: 24,032 sq km (9,279 sq miles)
Population: 1,300,000
Capital: Concord (pop 42,000)
Largest city: Manchester (pop 109,000)

 Maine

Area: 86,156 sq km (33,265 sq miles)
Population: 1,317,000
Capital: Augusta (pop 19,000)
Largest city: Portland (pop 64,000)

 Massachusetts

Area: 21,455 sq km (8,284 sq miles)
Population: 6,417,000
Capital and largest city: Boston (pop 569,000)

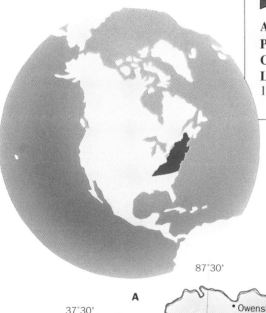

80°

Niag
Fa

D

82°30'
42°30'

Buffalo

Lake Erie

Erie

Jamesto

Oil City •

N

New Castle

Pittsburgh
Johnsto

40°

Wheeling•

Morgantown

Cumber

C

Parkersburg Clarksburg

Covington

B

Ohio

WEST VIRGINIA

Ashland •

Huntington

★ Charleston

Louisville
★ Frankfort

• Lexington

A

37°30'

• Owensboro

87°30'

KENTUCKY

• Danville

Beckley

Bluefield

Lynchbu

Roanoke

85°

Paducah •

*Lake
Barkley*

Mayfield

Bowling Green • Glasgow

Hopkinsville

Middlesboro

Mt Rogers
△ 1743m

Danv

22

Connecticut

Area: 12,997 sq km (5,018 sq miles)
Population: 3,504,000
Capital: Hartford (pop 125,000)
Largest city: Bridgeport (pop 140,000)

CANADA

MAINE

Caribou
Presque Isle

Mt Katahdin
△ 1605m

Chesuncook
Lake

Millinocket

Moosehead
Lake

Eastport

Bangor

Waterville

Bucksport

★ Augusta

Mount Desert
Island

Massena
Plattsburgh
Newport
Berlin

Lewiston

Ogdensburg

Lake
Champlain

Burlington

Mt Washington
1917m

Auburn

Westbrook

Portland

Mt Marcy △
1629m

Montpelier

White Mts

Biddeford

VERMONT

NEW
HAMPSHIRE

Adirondack Mts

Watertown

Rutland

Claremont

Rochester

Dover

Concord ★

Portsmouth

Glens Falls

Springfield

Manchester

Utica

Bennington

Brattleboro

Nashua

Lawrence

Rochester

Auburn Syracuse

Troy

Lowell

Cambridge

Finger Lakes

NEW YORK

Albany ★

Pittsfield MASSACHUSETTS

Boston

Brockton

Cape Cod

Ithaca

Springfield

Worcester

Catskill
Mts

Hartford

Providence

Binghamton

Fall River

New Bedford

Kingston

CONNECTICUT

RHODE
ISLAND

Nantucket I.

Poughkeepsie

Waterbury

Newport

Martha's
Vineyard

Scranton

New Haven

Williamsport

Wilkes-Barre

Bridgeport

Stamford

Paterson

Long Island

Newark
Jersey City
Elizabeth

New York City

Bethlehem

Allentown

NEW JERSEY

ATLANTIC
OCEAN

Reading

Trenton ★

Sunbury

PENNSYLVANIA

Harrisburg

Levittown

Norristown

Lancaster

Philadelphia

Camden

Chambersburg

York

Wilmington

Atlantic City

Hagerstown

Newark

Frederick

Vineland

Baltimore

Cape
May

MARYLAND

Dover ★

Winchester

Milford

Washington DC ★

Annapolis

DELAWARE

Arlington

Alexandria

Salisbury

Lexington Park

Fredericksburg

Charlottesville

VIRGINIA

James

Richmond ★

Chesapeake Bay

Petersburg

Hampton

Newport News

Norfolk

Portsmouth

Virginia Beach

St Lawrence

Mohawk

Hudson

Delaware

Susquehanna

Potomac

ke Ontario

miles
0   100
0   100
kilometres

Rhode Island

Area: 3,139 sq km (1,212 sq miles)
Population: 1,081,000
Capital and largest city:
Providence (pop 176,000)

Maryland

Area: 27,091 sq km (10,460 sq miles)
Population: 5,558,000
Capital: Annapolis (pop 36,000)
Largest city: Baltimore (pop 636,000)

Washington D.C.

Washington D.C., capital of the USA, is a federal district and is not part of a state. The D.C. stands for District of Columbia. Washington D.C. has an area of 179 sq km (69 sq miles) and a population of 554,000.

Delaware

Area: 5,294 sq km (2,045 sq miles)
Population: 830,000
Capital: Dover (pop 34,000)
Largest city: Wilmington (pop 73,000)

New Jersey

Area: 20,168 sq km (7,787 sq miles)
Population: 8,699,000
Capital: Trenton (pop 85,000)
Largest city: Newark (pop 280,000)

USA South-Eastern States

 Texas

Area: 691,207 sq km
(266,807 sq miles)
Population: 22,490,000
Capital: Austin (pop 682,000)
Largest city: Houston
(pop 2,013,000)

 Oklahoma

Area: 181,185 sq km
(69,955 sq miles)
Population: 3,524,000
Capital and largest city:
Oklahoma City (pop 528,000)

 Arkansas

Area: 137,754 sq km
(53,187 sq miles)
Population: 2,753,000
Capital and largest city:
Little Rock (pop 184,000)

Louisiana

Area: 123,677 sq km
(47,752 sq miles)
Population: 4,516,000
Capital: Baton Rouge (pop 224,000)
Largest city: New Orleans
(pop 454,000)

24

Tennessee

Area: 109,152 sq km
(42,144 sq miles)
Population: 5,901,000
Capital: Nashville (pop 546,000)
Largest city: Memphis
(pop 671,000)

North Carolina

Area: 136,412 sq km
(52,669 sq miles)
Population: 8,542,000
Capital: Raleigh (pop 326,000)
Largest city: Charlotte
(pop 543,000)

South Carolina

Area: 80,582 sq km
(31,113 sq miles)
Population: 4,198,000
Capital and largest city:
Columbia (pop 116,000)

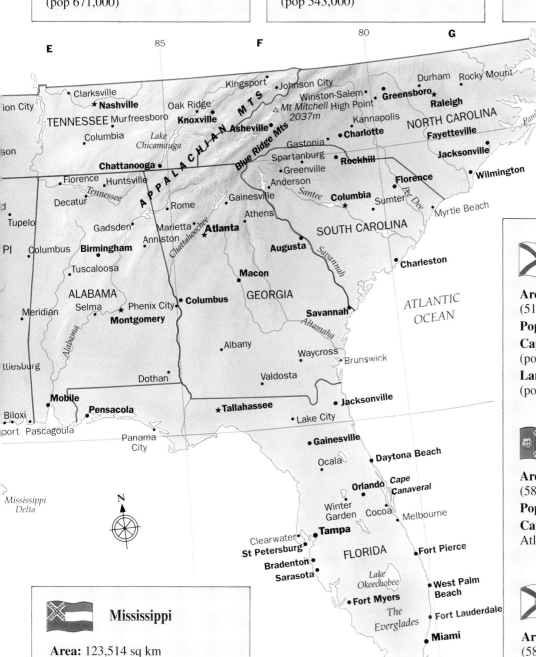

Alabama

Area: 133,915 sq km
(51,705 sq miles)
Population: 4,530,000
Capital: Montgomery
(pop 201,000)
Largest city: Birmingham
(pop 233,000)

Georgia

Area: 152,576 sq km
(58,910 sq miles)
Population: 8,829,000
Capital and largest city:
Atlanta (pop 419,000)

Florida

Area: 151,939 sq km
(58,664 sq miles)
Population: 17,397,000
Capital: Tallahassee (pop 157,000)
Largest city: Jacksonville
(pop 778 ,000)

Mississippi

Area: 123,514 sq km
(47,689 sq miles)
Population: 2,903,000
Capital and largest city:
Jackson (pop 179,000)

USA Mid-Western States

 North Dakota

Area: 183,117 sq km (70,702 sq miles)
Population: 634,000
Capital: Bismarck (pop 57,000)
Largest city: Fargo (pop 91,000)

 South Dakota

Area: 199,730 sq km (77,116 sq miles)
Population: 771,000
Capital: Pierre (pop 14,000)
Largest city: Sioux Falls (pop 137,000)

 Minnesota

Area: 224,329 sq km (86,614 sq miles)
Population: 5,101,000
Capital: St. Paul (pop 277,000)
Largest city: Minneapolis (pop 374,000)

 Nebraska

Area: 200,349 sq km (77,355 sq miles)
Population: 1,747,000
Capital: Lincoln (pop 236,000)
Largest city: Omaha (pop 409,000)

 Kansas

Area: 213,096 sq km (82,277 sq miles)
Population: 2,736,000
Capital: Topeka (pop 122,000)
Largest city: Wichita (pop 354,000)

Iowa

Area: 145,752 sq km (56,275 sq miles)
Population: 2,954,000
Capital and largest city: Des Moines (pop 194,000)

 Missouri

Area: 180,514 sq km (69,697 sq miles)
Population: 5,755,000
Capital: Jefferson City (pop 39,000)
Largest city: Kansas City (pop 444,000)

 Wisconsin

Area: 171,496 sq km (66,215 sq miles)
Population: 5,509,000
Capital: Madison (pop 220,000)
Largest city: Milwaukee (pop 584,000)

 Michigan

Area: 251,493 sq km (97,102 sq miles)
Population: 10,113,000
Capital: Lansing (pop 117,000)
Largest city: Detroit (pop 900,000)

 Ohio

Area: 115,998 sq km (44,787 sq miles)
Population: 11,459,000
Capital and largest city: Columbus (pop 730,000)

 Indiana

Area: 94,309 sq km (36,413 sq miles)
Population: 6,238,000
Capital and largest city: Indianapolis (pop 784,000)

Illinois

Area: 149,885 sq km (57,871 sq miles)
Population: 12,714,000
Capital: Springfield (pop 115,000)
Largest city: Chicago (pop 2,862,000)

USA Western States

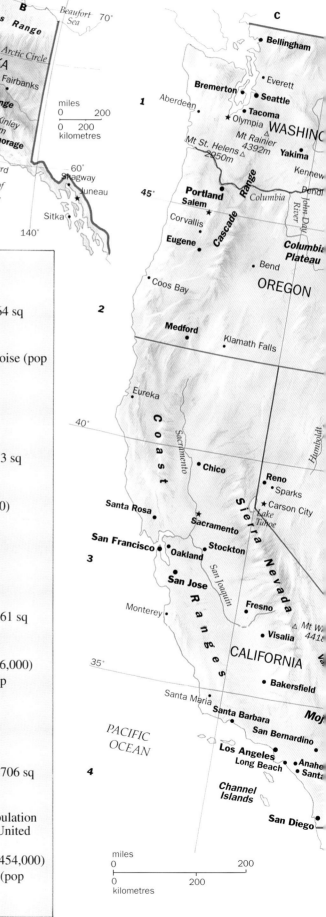

Hawaii

Area: 16,760 sq km (6,471 sq miles)
Population: 1,263,000
Capital and largest city: Honolulu (pop 380,000)

Alaska

Area: 1,530,693 sq km (591,004 sq miles)
Population: 655,000
Capital: Juneau (pop 31,000)
Largest city: Anchorage (pop 273,000)

Washington

Area: 176,479 sq km (68,139 sq miles)
Population: 6,204,000
Capital: Olympia (pop 44,000)
Largest city: Seattle (pop 571,000)

Idaho

Area: 216,430 sq km (83,564 sq miles)
Population: 1,393,000
Capital and largest city: Boise (pop 190,000)

Oregon

Area: 251,418 sq km (97,073 sq miles)
Population: 3,595,000
Capital: Salem (pop 146,000)
Largest city: Portland (pop 533,000)

Nevada

Area: 286,352 sq km (110,561 sq miles)
Population: 2,335,000
Capital: Carson City (pop 56,000)
Largest city: Las Vegas (pop 535,000)

California

Area: 411,047 sq km (158,706 sq miles)
Population: 35,894,000 (California has a larger population than any other state in the United States)
Capital: Sacramento (pop 454,000)
Largest city: Los Angeles (pop 3,846,000)

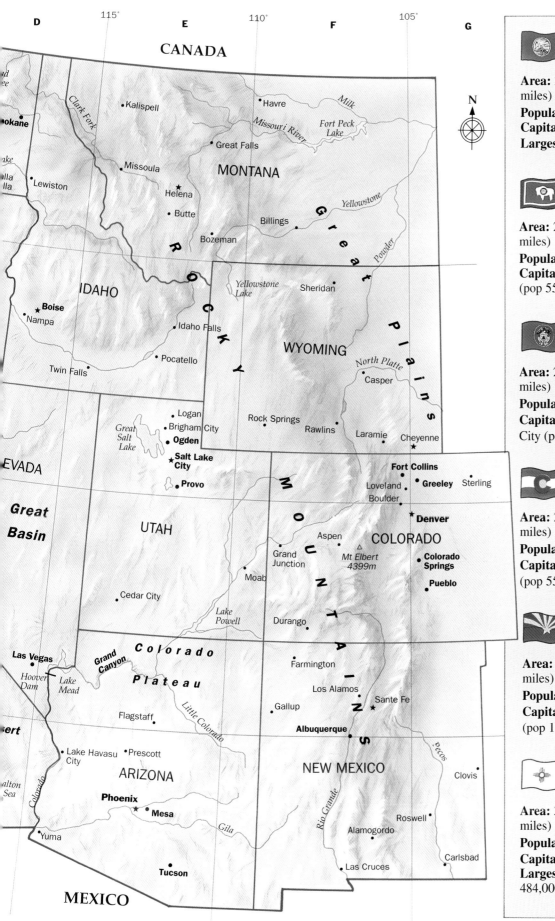

D · 115° · E · 110° · F · 105° · G

CANADA

N

MONTANA

Kalispell
Havre
Milk
Missouri River
Fort Peck Lake
Great Falls
Missoula
Helena
Butte
Billings
Bozeman
Yellowstone
Great
Powder

IDAHO
ROCKY

Yellowstone Lake
Sheridan

Boise
Nampa
Idaho Falls

WYOMING
North Platte
Casper

Twin Falls
Pocatello

Plains

Logan
Brigham City
Rock Springs
Rawlins
Laramie
Cheyenne

Great Salt Lake
Ogden
Salt Lake City
Provo

EVADA

Fort Collins
Loveland · Greeley · Sterling
Boulder

Great Basin

UTAH
MOUNTAINS

Denver
Aspen
COLORADO

Grand Junction
Mt Elbert 4399m
Colorado Springs

Moab
Pueblo

Cedar City

Lake Powell
Durango

Las Vegas
Colorado
Grand Canyon
Hoover Dam
Lake Mead
Plateau

Farmington
Los Alamos
Santa Fe
Gallup

Flagstaff
Little Colorado
Albuquerque

ert
Lake Havasu City · Prescott
NEW MEXICO
Clovis

alton Sea
ARIZONA
Pecos

Phoenix · Mesa
Roswell
Gila
Alamogordo

Yuma
Rio Grande
Carlsbad

Tucson
Las Cruces

MEXICO

 Montana

Area: 380,347 sq km (147,046 sq miles)
Population: 927,000
Capital: Helena (pop 27,000)
Largest city: Billings (pop 97,000)

 Wyoming

Area: 253,324 sq km (97,809 sq miles)
Population: 507,000
Capital and largest city: Cheyenne (pop 55,000)

 Utah

Area: 219,887 sq km (84,899 sq miles)
Population: 2,389,000
Capital and largest city: Salt Lake City (pop 179,000)

 Colorado

Area: 269,594 sq km (104,091 sq miles)
Population: 4,601,000
Capital and largest city: Denver (pop 557,000)

 Arizona

Area: 295,259 sq km (114,000 sq miles)
Population: 5,744,000
Capital and largest city: Phoenix (pop 1,418,000)

 New Mexico

Area: 314,924 sq km (121,593 sq miles)
Population: 1,903,000
Capital: Santa Fe (pop 68,000)
Largest city: Albuquerque (pop 484,000)

29

Mexico and Central America

A   115°   B   110°   C   105°   D   100°   E

Tijuana
Mexicali
Ensenada
1
Colorado

30°

Ciudad Juárez

UNITED STATES

N

Hermosillo
2
Chihuahua
Rio Bravo del Norte
Piedras Negras

Ciudad Obrégon

Nuevo Laredo

Baja California

Gulf of California

Hidalgo Del Parral

Reynosa
Nuevo Laredo

25°

Los Mochis
• Guasave

Sierra Madre Occidental

Sierra Madre Oriental

Monterrey
Matamoros

Torreón
Saltillo

Culiacán   **M E X I C O**

• Durango

Ciudad Victoria

Mazatlán
3

Tampico

Aguascalientes   San Luis Potosi

• Tepic

• León

Guadalajara
Irapuato   Querétaro

Celaya   Pachuca

20°

Uruapan   Mexico City   *Citlaltépetl* Jal En
• Colima   Morelia   *Volcano 5700m* △
Toluca•   Verac
4   Cuernavaca•   **Puebla**   Oriz.
Balsas   *Popocatépetl Volcano 5452m*

PACIFIC OCEAN

Sierra Madre del Sur

Acapulco•   Oaxa•

15°

MEXICO
Area: 1,972,547 sq km (761,605 sq miles)
Highest point: Citlaltépetl (also called Orizaba) 5,700m (18,701ft)
Population: 106,203,000
Capital and largest city: Mexico City (pop 8,520,000; pop of metropolitan area 18,660,000)
Other cities:
Guadalajara (3,697,000)
Monterrey (3,267,000)
Puebla (1,888,000)
Official language: Spanish
Religion: Christianity (95.9%)
Main products: Oil, silver, machinery and other manufactures, farm products
Currency: Mexican Peso
Government: Federal republic (official name: United States of Mexico)

BELIZE
Area: 22,965 sq km (8,867 sq miles)
Population: 281,000
Capital: Belmopan (pop 9,000)
Largest city: Belize City (pop 50,000)

GUATEMALA
Area: 108,889 sq km (42,042 sq miles)
Population: 12,014,000
Capital and largest city: Guatemala City (pop 951,000)
Currency: Quetzal

EL SALVADOR
Area: 21,041 sq km (8,124 sq miles)
Population: 6,705,000
Capital and largest city: San Salvador (pop 1,424,000)
Official language: Spanish
Currency: Colón, U.S. Dollar

HONDURAS
Area: 112,088 sq km (43,277 sq miles)
Population: 7,168,000
Capital and largest city: Tegucigalpa (pop 1,007,000)
Currency: Lempira

NICARAGUA
Area: 130,000 sq km (50,193 sq miles)
Population: 5,465,000
Capital and largest city: Managua (pop 1,098,000)
Official language: Spanish
Currency: Córdoba

COSTA RICA
Area: 50,700 sq km (19,575 sq miles)
Population: 4,016,000
Capital and largest city: San José (pop 1,085,000)
Official language: Spanish
Currency: Colón

PANAMA
Area: 77, 082 sq km (29,762 sq miles)
Population: 3,140,000
Capital and largest city: Panama City (pop 930,000)
Official language: Spanish
Currency: Balboa

South America (Political)

COLOMBIA

Area: 1,138,914 sq km (439,747 sq miles)

Population: 42,954,000

Capital and largest city: Bogotá (pop 7,290,000)

Currency: Colombian Peso

VENEZUELA

Area: 912,050 sq km (352,145 sq miles)

Population: 25,375,000

Capital and largest city: Caracas (pop 3,226,000)

Currency: Bolivar

ECUADOR

Area: 283,561 sq km (109,484 sq miles)

Population: 13,364,000

Capital: Quito (pop 1,451,000)

Currency: U.S. Dollar

PERU

Area: 1,285,216 sq km (496,225 sq miles)

Population: 27,926,000

Capital and largest city: Lima (pop 7,899,000)

Currency: Sol

BOLIVIA

Area: 1,098,581 sq km (424,165 sq miles)

Population: 8,858,000

Capital and largest city: La Paz (pop 1,477,000)

Currency: Boliviano

CHILE

Area: 756,945 sq km (292,258 sq miles)

Population: 15,981,000

Capital and largest city: Santiago (pop 5,478,000)

Currency: Chilean Peso

Caracas
VENEZUELA
Bogotá
COLOMBIA
Quito
ECUADOR
PERU
Lima
La Paz
BOLIVI
CHILE
Santiago

GUYANA
Area: 214,969 sq km (83,000 sq miles)
Population: 765,000
Capital: Georgetown (pop 231,000)
Currency: Guyana Dollar

SURINAM
Area: 163,265 sq km (63,037 sq miles)
Population: 438,000
Capital: Paramaribo (pop 253,000)
Currency: Surinam Dollar

FRENCH GUIANA
Area: 90,000 sq km (34,749 sq miles)
Population: 191,000
Capital: Cayenne (pop 50,000)
Currency: Euro

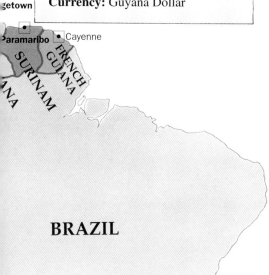

getown
• Paramaribo • Cayenne

FRENCH GUIANA

SURINAM

BRAZIL

• Brasilia

RAGUAY

• Asunción

URUGUAY

• Montevideo

os
s

RGENTINA

BRAZIL
Area: 8,511,965 sq km (3,286,488 sq miles)
Population: 186,113,000
Capital: Brasilia (pop 3,099,000)
Largest cities: São Paulo (17,099,000) metropolitan area) Rio de Janeiro (10,803,000) Belo Horizonte (4,659,000)
Official language: Portuguese
Currency: Real

PARAGUAY
Area: 406,752 sq km (157,048 sq miles)
Population: 6,348,000
Capital and largest city: Asunción (pop 1,639,000)
Official language: Spanish
Currency: Guarani

ARGENTINA
Area: 2,766,889 sq km (1,068,302 sq miles)
Highest point: Aconcagua 6,960m (22,831ft)
Population: 39,538,000
Capital and largest city: Buenos Aires (pop 2,982,000; metropolitan area 13,047,000)
Official language: Spanish
Religion: Christianity
Currency: Argentine Peso

URUGUAY
Area: 176,215 sq km (68,037 sq miles)
Population: 3,416,000
Capital and largest city: Montevideo (pop 1,341,000)
Currency: Uruguayan Peso

FALKLAND ISLANDS (U.K.)
Area: 12,173 sq km (4,700 sq miles)
Population: 3,000
Capital: Stanley

lkland Islands (U.K.)
Stanley

...pe

...nd smallest continent; only Australia is smaller. It
...ts of the former Soviet Union including Belarus,
...ova, Ukraine, Estonia, Latvia, Lithuania and part of the
Russian Federation, the world's largest country and the only
country located in more than one continent.

The highest peak in Europe is Mount Elbrus in the Caucasus
Mountains which form part of the border between Europe and Asia.
The longest river, the Volga, is in the Russian Federation and flows
into the Caspian Sea.

Europe also contains the world's smallest country, Vatican City,
which is situated in Rome, the capital of Italy.

Europe's population of about 700 million, including the European
part of Russia, is greater than that of any other continent except Asia
and Africa.

France, Belgium and Switzerland

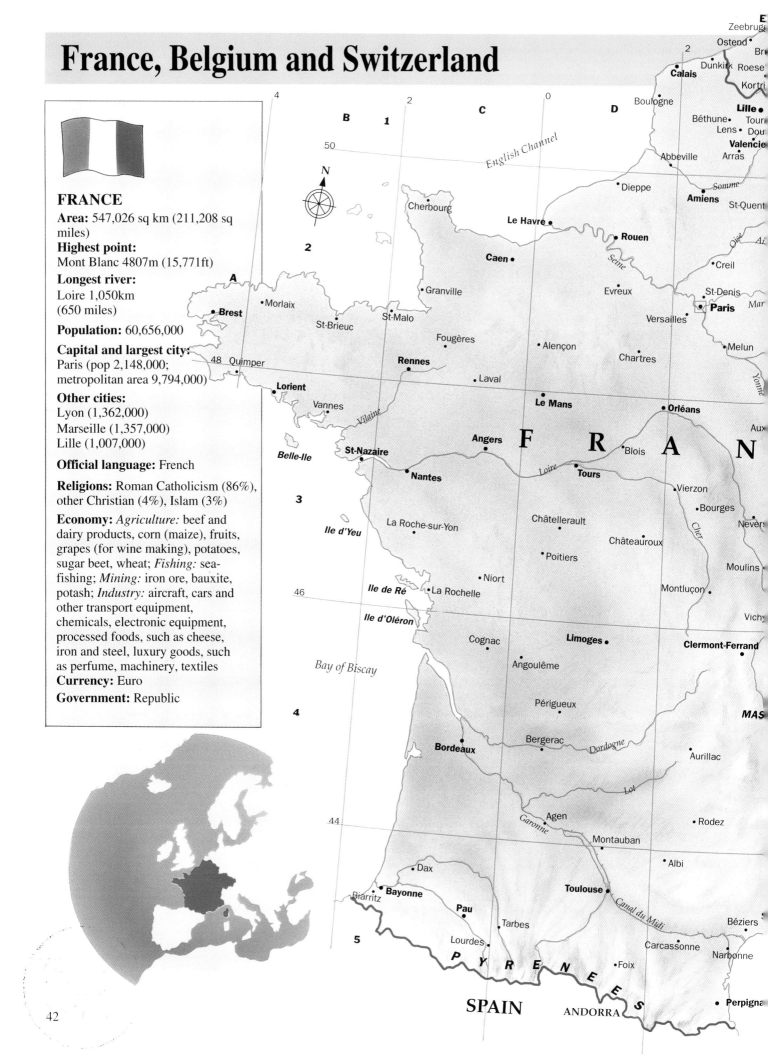

FRANCE

Area: 547,026 sq km (211,208 sq miles)

Highest point:
Mont Blanc 4807m (15,771ft)

Longest river:
Loire 1,050km
(650 miles)

Population: 60,656,000

Capital and largest city:
Paris (pop 2,148,000;
metropolitan area 9,794,000)

Other cities:
Lyon (1,362,000)
Marseille (1,357,000)
Lille (1,007,000)

Official language: French

Religions: Roman Catholicism (86%),
other Christian (4%), Islam (3%)

Economy: *Agriculture:* beef and
dairy products, corn (maize), fruits,
grapes (for wine making), potatoes,
sugar beet, wheat; *Fishing:* sea-
fishing; *Mining:* iron ore, bauxite,
potash; *Industry:* aircraft, cars and
other transport equipment,
chemicals, electronic equipment,
processed foods, such as cheese,
iron and steel, luxury goods, such
as perfume, machinery, textiles

Currency: Euro

Government: Republic

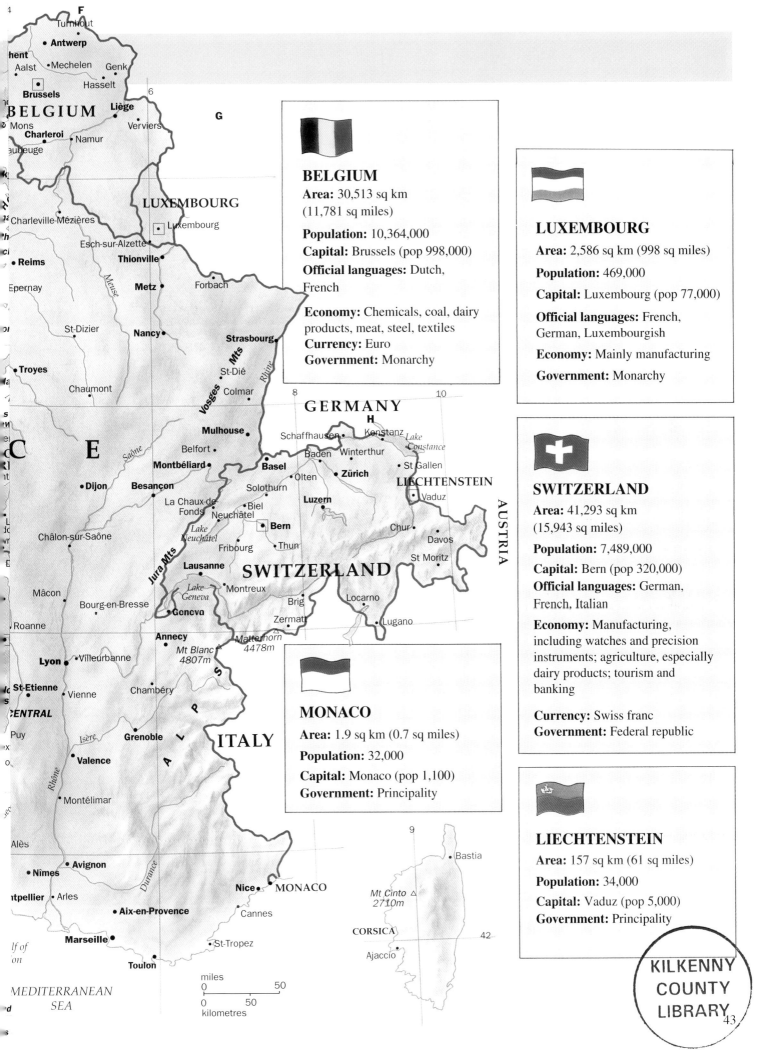

BELGIUM
- Turnhout
- **Antwerp**
- Aalst • Mechelen • Genk
- hent
- **Brussels** □
- Hasselt
- **BELGIUM**
- **Liège**
- Mons
- **Charleroi** • Namur
- Verviers
- aubeuge
- Charleville-Mézières

G

LUXEMBOURG
- □ Luxembourg
- Esch-sur-Alzette

- Reims
- **Thionville**
- Épernay
- **Metz** • Forbach
- St-Dizier
- **Nancy**
- Troyes
- Chaumont
- **Strasbourg**
- St-Dié
- Colmar

Mts Vosges · Rhine

8

GERMANY **10**

H

- **Mulhouse**
- Schaffhausen • Konstanz · *Lake Constance*
- Belfort
- Baden • Winterthur
- **Montbéliard**
- **Basel** • St Gallen
- Olten • **Zürich**
- C E
- Saône
- **Dijon**
- **Besançon**
- Solothurn
- **LIECHTENSTEIN**
- La Chaux-de-Fonds • Biel
- **Luzern**
- □ Vaduz
- Neuchâtel
- □ **Bern**
- Chur
- *Lake Neuchâtel*
- Davos
- Fribourg
- • Thun
- St Moritz
- Jura Mts
- **Lausanne**
- **SWITZERLAND**
- *Lake Geneva*
- Montreux
- **AUSTRIA**
- Mâcon
- Brig
- Locarno
- Bourg-en-Bresse
- **Geneva**
- Zermatt
- Lugano
- Roanne
- *Matterhorn 4478m*
- Annecy
- **Lyon** • Villeurbanne
- *Mt Blanc 4807m*
- St-Étienne
- Vienne
- Chambéry
- **ITALY**
- CENTRAL
- A L P S
- Puy
- Isère
- **Grenoble**
- x
- o
- **Valence**
- Rhône
- Montélimar
- Alès
- • **Avignon**
- • Nîmes
- Durance
- **Nice** **MONACO**
- ntpellier • Arles
- Cannes
- **9**
- • Bastia
- **Aix-en-Provence**
- *Mt Cinto 2710m*
- **Marseille**
- St-Tropez
- **42**
- **CORSICA**
- Toulon
- Ajaccio
- *MEDITERRANEAN SEA*
- lf of on

BELGIUM
Area: 30,513 sq km (11,781 sq miles)

Population: 10,364,000
Capital: Brussels (pop 998,000)
Official languages: Dutch, French

Economy: Chemicals, coal, dairy products, meat, steel, textiles
Currency: Euro
Government: Monarchy

LUXEMBOURG
Area: 2,586 sq km (998 sq miles)

Population: 469,000

Capital: Luxembourg (pop 77,000)

Official languages: French, German, Luxembourgish

Economy: Mainly manufacturing

Government: Monarchy

SWITZERLAND
Area: 41,293 sq km (15,943 sq miles)

Population: 7,489,000

Capital: Bern (pop 320,000)
Official languages: German, French, Italian

Economy: Manufacturing, including watches and precision instruments; agriculture, especially dairy products; tourism and banking

Currency: Swiss franc
Government: Federal republic

MONACO
Area: 1.9 sq km (0.7 sq miles)

Population: 32,000

Capital: Monaco (pop 1,100)

Government: Principality

LIECHTENSTEIN
Area: 157 sq km (61 sq miles)

Population: 34,000

Capital: Vaduz (pop 5,000)

Government: Principality

miles
0   50

0   50
kilometres

Spain and Portugal

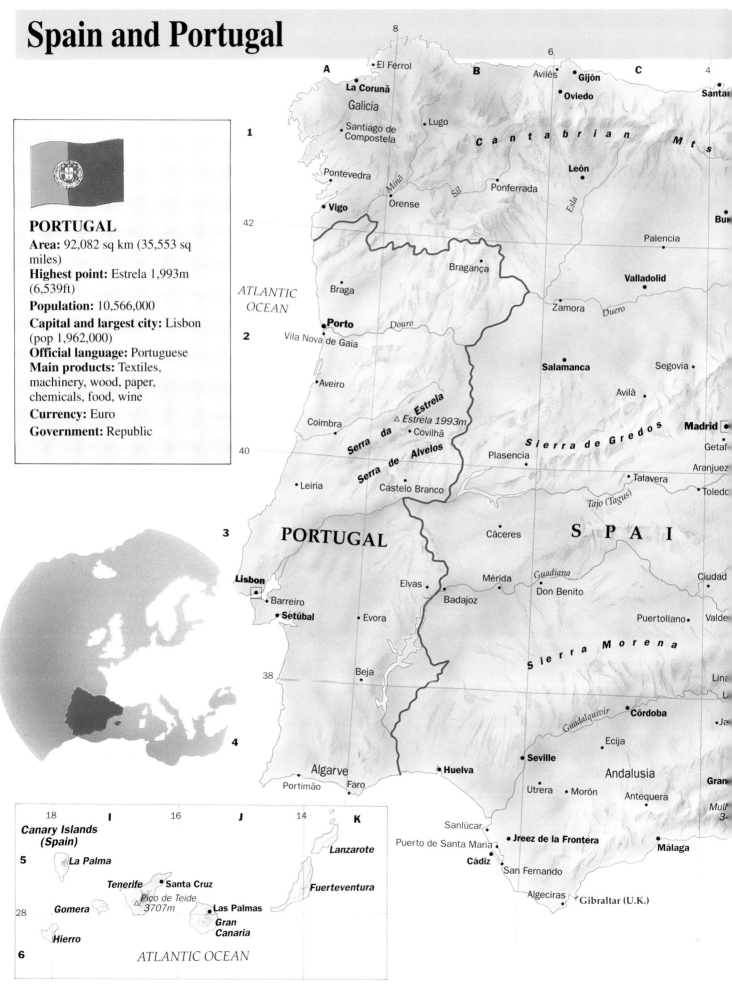

PORTUGAL

Area: 92,082 sq km (35,553 sq miles)

Highest point: Estrela 1,993m (6,539ft)

Population: 10,566,000

Capital and largest city: Lisbon (pop 1,962,000)

Official language: Portuguese

Main products: Textiles, machinery, wood, paper, chemicals, food, wine

Currency: Euro

Government: Republic

ATLANTIC OCEAN

8
6
4

A
El Ferrol
La Corunã
Galicia
Santiago de Compostela
Lugo
B
Avilés
Gijón
Oviedo
C
Santar

1

Pontevedra
Vigo
Minõ
Orense
Sil
Ponferrada
Cantabrian Mts
León
Esla
Bu

42
Palencia

Bragança
Valladolid

Braga
Zamora
Duero

Porto
Douro
Vila Nova de Gaia
2
Salamanca
Segovia

Aveiro
Avilà
Madrid
Getaf

Coimbra
Serra da
Estrela
△ Estrela 1993m
Covilhã
Sierra de Gredos
Aranjuez

40
Serra de Alvelos
Plasencia
Talavera
Toledo

Leiria
Castelo Branco
Tajo (Tagus)

3
PORTUGAL
Cáceres
S P A I
Ciudad

Lisbon
Elvas
Mérida
Guadiana
Don Benito

Barreiro
Badajoz
Puertollano
Valde

Setúbal
Evora
Sierra Morena

38
Beja
Lina
U

Guadalquivir
Córdoba
Ja

4
Ecija

Algarve
Portimão
Faro
Huelva
Seville
Andalusia
Utrera
Morón
Antequera
Gran
Mull
3

18
I
16
J
14
K
Sanlúcar
Puerto de Santa Maria
Jreez de la Frontera
Málaga

Canary Islands (Spain)

Lanzarote
Cádiz
San Fernando

5
La Palma
Fuerteventura
Algeciras
Gibraltar (U.K.)

Tenerife
Santa Cruz

28
Gomera
△ Pico de Teide 3707m
Las Palmas
Gran Canaria

Hierro

6
ATLANTIC OCEAN

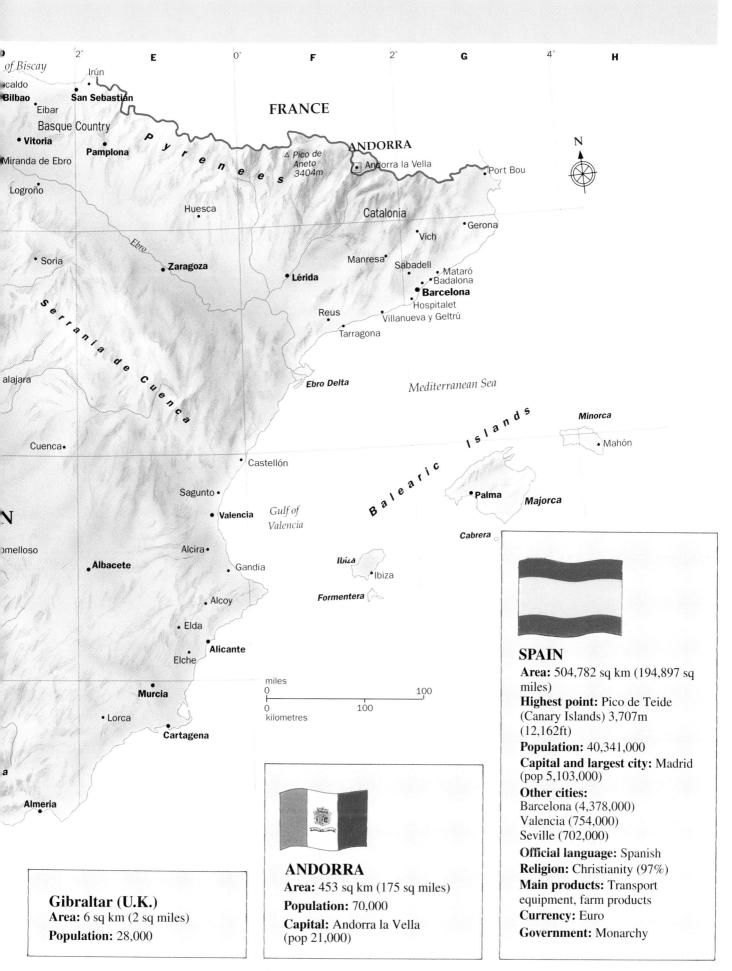

of Biscay

2° E 0° F 2° G 4° H

Irún
acaldo
Bilbao **San Sebastián**
Eibar

FRANCE

Basque Country

ANDORRA

Vitoria

Pamplona

Miranda de Ebro

△ Pico de
Aneto
3404m

Andorra la Vella

Port Bou

Logroño

Huesca

N

Catalonia

Vich
Gerona

Soria

Ebro

Zaragoza

Manresa
Sabadell
Lérida
Mataró
Badalona
Barcelona
Hospitalet
Villanueva y Geltrú

Reus

Serrania de Cuenca

alajara

Tarragona

Ebro Delta

Mediterranean Sea

Cuenca

Castellón

Balearic Islands

Minorca

Mahón

Sagunto

Palma
Majorca

Gulf of
Valencia

Valencia

Cabrera

omelloso

Alcira

Ibiza

Gandia

Ibiza

Albacete

Alcoy

Formentera

Elda

Alicante

Elche

miles
0   100

Murcia

0   100
kilometres

Lorca

Cartagena

a

Almeria

SPAIN
Area: 504,782 sq km (194,897 sq miles)
Highest point: Pico de Teide (Canary Islands) 3,707m (12,162ft)
Population: 40,341,000
Capital and largest city: Madrid (pop 5,103,000)
Other cities:
Barcelona (4,378,000)
Valencia (754,000)
Seville (702,000)
Official language: Spanish
Religion: Christianity (97%)
Main products: Transport equipment, farm products
Currency: Euro
Government: Monarchy

Gibraltar (U.K.)
Area: 6 sq km (2 sq miles)
Population: 28,000

ANDORRA
Area: 453 sq km (175 sq miles)
Population: 70,000
Capital: Andorra la Vella (pop 21,000)

North-Western Europe

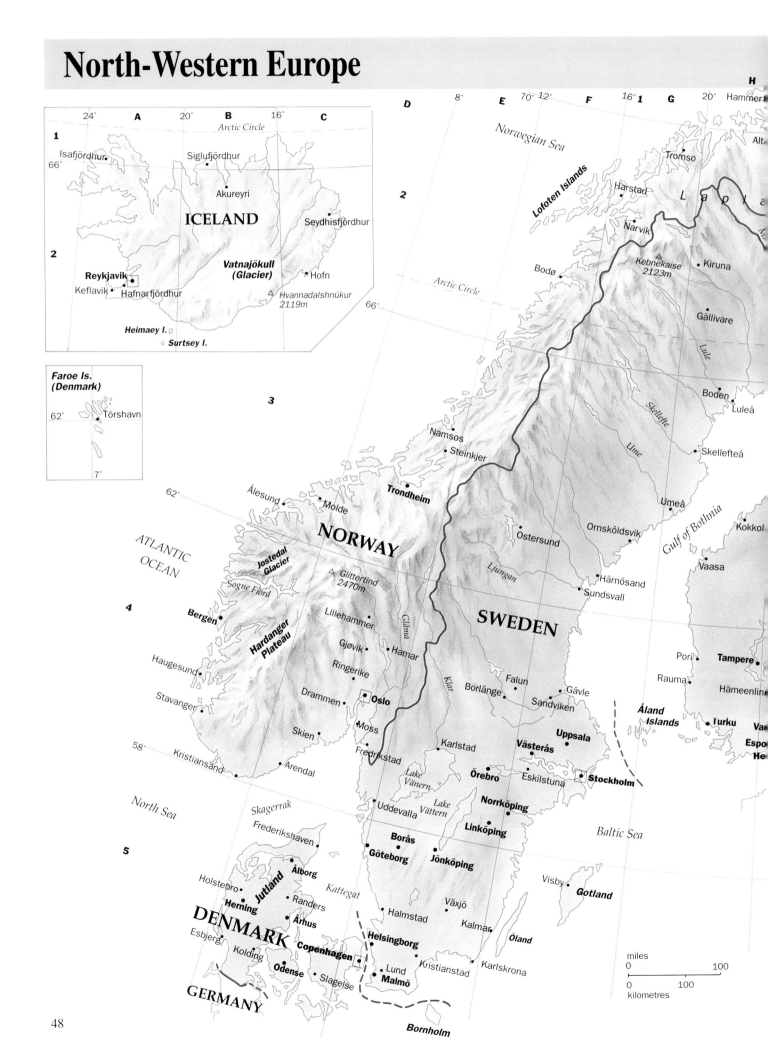

A   **B**   **C**   **D**   **E**   **F**   **G**   **H**

24°   20°   16°   8°   70° 12°   16° 1   20°   Hammer

1

Arctic Circle

Isafjördhur   Siglufjördhur

66°

Akureyri

ICELAND   Seydhisfjördhur

2

Reykjavik   *Vatnajökull*   Hofn
(Glacier)

Keflavik

Hafnarfjördhur   △ *Hvannadalshnúkur*
    2119m

66°

Heimaey I. □

○ *Surtsey I.*

*Faroe Is.
(Denmark)*

62°   Tórshavn

7°

Norwegian Sea

Alt.

Tromso

Lofoten Islands   Harstad   *L*

2

Narvik

Bodø   Kebnekaise   Kiruna
    △ 2123m

Arctic Circle

66°   Gällivare

Lule

3   Boden

Namsos   *Skellefte*   Luleå

62°   Steinkjer

Ålesund   **Trondheim**   Skellefteå

Molde   *Ume*

NORWAY   Östersund   Örnsköldsvik   Umeå   *Gulf of Bothnia*   Kokkol

*ATLANTIC
OCEAN*

*Jostedal
Glacier*   △ Glittertind   *Ljungan*
    2470m

Sogne Fiord   Härnösand   Vaasa

4   **Bergen**   Lillehammer   Sundsvall

*Hardanger
Plateau*   Gjøvik   Hamar   **SWEDEN**   Pori   **Tampere**

Haugesund   Ringerike   *Glåma*   Falun   Rauma   Hämeenlin

Stavanger   Drammen   □ **Oslo**   *Klar*   Börlänge   Gävle   *Åland
Islands*

Moss   Sandviken   **Turku**   Va

Skien   **Uppsala**   **Espo**

58°   Kristiansand   Fredrikstad   Karlstad   **Västerås**   **He**

Arendal   *Lake
Vänern*   **Örebro**   Eskilstuna   □ **Stockholm**

North Sea   *Skagerrak*   Uddevalla   *Lake
Vättern*   **Norrköping**   *Baltic Sea*

Frederikshaven   **Linköping**

5   **Borås**

Göteborg   **Jönköping**   Visby   **Gotland**

Holstebro   **Ålborg**   *Kattegat*

Jutland   Randers   Växjö

Herning   Halmstad   Kalmar   **Öland**

DENMARK   **Århus**

Esbjerg   **Helsingborg**

Kolding   **Copenhagen** □   Kristianstad   Karlskrona

Odense   Slagelse   Lund

GERMANY   **Malmö**

Bornholm

miles
0   100
0   100
kilometres

Vadso

Lake
Inari

N

Kemi

aniemi Kemijärvi

ulu

RUSSIA

Lake
ärvi

Kajaani

INLAND

Lake
Pielinen

Kuopio
Lake
Kallavesi Joensuu
Lake
Orivesi
vväskylä

Lake
Kokon Selka

inne

nti Lappeenranta
Kouvola

Kotka

of Finland

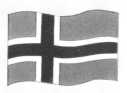

ICELAND
Area: 103,000 sq km (39,769 sq miles)
Population: 297,000
Capital: Reykjavik (pop 184,000)
Main export: Fish and fish products
Currency: Icelandic Króna
Government: Republic

NORWAY
Area: 324,219 sq km (125,182 sq miles)
Population: 4,593,000
Capital: Oslo (pop 795,000)
Main export: Oil and natural gas
Currency: Krone
Government: Monarchy

SWEDEN
Area: 449,964 sq km (173,732 sq miles)
Population: 9,002,000
Capital: Stockholm (pop 1,697,000)
Main exports: Machinery and transport equipment, wood and wood pulp, chemicals
Currency: Swedish Krona
Government: Monarchy

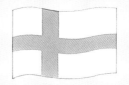

FINLAND
Area: 337,032 sq km (130,129 sq miles)
Population: 5,223,000
Capital: Helsinki (pop 1,075,000)
Main exports: Metal products and machinery, paper, wood and wood products
Currency: Euro
Government: Republic

DENMARK
Area: 43,069 sq km (16,629 sq miles) not including the Faroe Islands and Greenland
Population: 5,432,000
Capital: Copenhagen (pop 1,066,000)
Main exports: Machinery and instruments, food products
Currency: Danish Krone
Government: Monarchy

Germany and North-Central Europe

North Sea

Baltic Sea

NETHERLANDS

GERMANY

BELGIUM

FRANCE

SWITZERLAND

ITALY

AUSTRIA

CZECH REPUBLIC

SLOVENIA

CROATIA

Flensburg
Kiel
Neumunster
Stralsund
Rostock
Lübeck
Wismar
Schwerin
Hamburg
Slupsk
Koszalin
Bremerhaven
Bremen
Oldenburg
Osnabrück
Hanover
Neustrelitz
Szczecin
Bydgoszcz
Pila
Inowrocl
Poznan
Berlin
Potsdam
Braunschweig
Saltzgitter
Magdeburg
Halberstadt
Dessau
Halle
Leipzig
Cottbus
Görlitz
Legnica
Wroclaw
Kalisz
Opole
Walbrzych
Ostr
Erfurt
Gera
Dresden
Chemnitz
Zwickau
Plauen
Usti nad Labem
Liberec
Hradec Králové
Kladno
Prague
Pardubice
CZECH
Plzen
Pribram
Olomouc
Jihlava
Brno
Znojmo
České Budějovice
Krems
Vienna
Linz
Wels
Steyr
St. Pölten
Bratislava
Salzburg
Lake Neusiedler
Wiener Neustadt
Győr
Innsbruck
Gross Glockner 3798m
Leoben
Szombathely
Graz
Székesfehérvar
Villach
Klagenfurt
Lake Balaton
Nagykanizsa
Frisian Islands
Leeuwarden
Wilhelmshaven
Haarlem
Amsterdam
The Hague
Enschede
Rotterdam
Utrecht
Arnhem
Breda
Eindhoven
Münster
Bielefeld
Duisburg
Dortmund
Essen
Krefeld
Wuppertal
Düsseldorf
Kassel
Aachen
Cologne
Bonn
Koblenz
Giessen
Eifel
Wiesbaden
Frankfurt am Main
Trier
Mainz
Offenbach
Schweinfurt
Bamberg
Darmstadt
Würzburg
Mannheim
Heidelburg
Nuremburg
Saarbrücken
Karlsruhe
Heilbronn
Regensburg
Stuttgart
Freiburg
Ulm
Augsburg
Ravensburg
Munich
Dornbirn
Maastricht
Isselmeer
Maas
Mosel
Rhine
Black Forest
Lake Constance
Weser
Harz Mts
Thuringian Forest
Elbe
Ore Mts
Bohemian Forest
Main
Danube
Inn
Enns
Mur
Drava
Váh
Alps
Sudeten Mts
Oder
Neisse
Warta

52
48
6
10
14
A · B · C · D · G
1
2
3

NETHERLANDS

Area: 40,844 sq km (15,770 sq miles)

Population: 16,407,000

Capital: Amsterdam (pop 1,145,000)

Official language: Dutch

Main exports: Machinery and transport equipment, food, chemicals, mineral fuels, including natural gas, metals and metal products

Currency: Euro

Government: Monarchy

RUSSIA   LITHUANIA

•Elblag

Olsztyn

Lomza   Bialystok

Wloclawek

ck *Vistula*   *Bug*   BELARUS

Warsaw   •Siedlce

POLAND

Lódź

•Piotrków   Pulawy
Radom   •Lublin

•Kielce
Czestochowa   Zamość

Vistula   *San*
•wice   Jaroslaw
Kraków   Rzeszów•
Przemysl

Carpathian Mts

△ Gerlachovka Stit
2655m

SLOVAKIA   Košice   UKRAINE

Miskolc

Debrecen

•udapest   *Tisza*
•UNGARY

•cskémét   Békéscsaba

Hódmezövásárhely   ROMANIA
Szeged •

RBIA

miles
0   100
0   100
kilometres

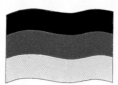

GERMANY

Area: 356,755 sq km (137,744 sq miles)

Population: 82,431,000

Capital: Berlin (pop 3,327,000)

Other cities:
Hamburg (2,670,000)
Munich, or München (2,300,000)
Cologne, or Köln (963,000)
Frankfurt am Main (644,000)

Official language: German

Religions: Protestant (43%), Roman Catholic (35%)

Economy: *Agriculture:* barley wheat, rye, potatoes, sugar beet; *Fishing:* cod, herring; *Mining:* coal, lignite, iron, potash; *Industry:* machinery and transport equipment, motor vehicles, chemicals and chemical products

Currency: Euro

Government: Republic

CZECH REPUBLIC

Area: 78,864 sq km (30,450 sq miles)

Population: 10,241,000

Capital: Prague (pop 1,170,000)

Currency: Czech Koruna

SLOVAKIA

Area: 49,035 sq km (18,933 sq miles)

Population: 5,431,000

Capital: Bratislava (pop 425,000)

Currency: Slovak Koruna

POLAND

Area: 312,677 sq km (120,725 sq miles)

Population: 38,558,000

Capital: Warsaw (pop 2,200,000)

Main exports: Machinery and transport equipment

Currency: Zloty

Government: Republic

AUSTRIA

Area: 83,849 sq km (32,374 sq miles)

Population: 8,185,000

Capital: Vienna (pop 2,179,000)

Main exports: Machinery and transport equipment

Currency: Euro

Government: Republic

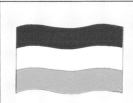

HUNGARY

Area: 93,030 sq km (35,919 sq miles)

Population: 10,007,000

Capital: Budapest (pop 1,708,000)

Main exports: Machinery and transport equipment

Currency: Forint

Government: Republic

Italy and South-Eastern Europe

ITALY

Area: 301,225 sq km (116,304 sq miles)
Population: 55,103,000
Capital: Rome (pop 2,665,000)
Other large cities: Milan (4,183,000)
Naples (2,995,000),Turin (1,247,000)
Official language: Italian
Religion: Roman Catholic (90%)
Currency: Euro

VATICAN CITY
(in Rome)
Area: 44 hectares (109 acres)
Population: 1,000

SAN MARINO

Area: 61 sq km (24 sq miles)
Population: 29,000
Capital: San Marino
(pop 4,500)

SLOVENIA

Area: 20,250 sq km (7,820 sq miles)
Population: 2,011,000
Capital: Ljubljana (pop 256,000)

CROATIA

Area: 56,540 sq km (21,829 sq miles)
Population: 4,495,000
Capital: Zagreb (pop 688,000)

SERBIA

Area: 88,357 sq km (34,115 sq miles)
Population: 10,106,000
Capital: Belgrade (pop 1,594,000)

MONTENEGRO

Area: 13,812 sq km (5,334 sq miles)
Population: 723,000
Capital: Podgorica (pop 160,000)

BOSNIA & HERCEGOVINA

Area: 51,129 sq km (19,741 sq miles)
Population: 4,430,000
Capital: Sarajevo (pop 579,000)

MALTA

Area: 316 sq km (122 sq miles)
Population: 398,000
Capital: Valletta (pop 83,000)

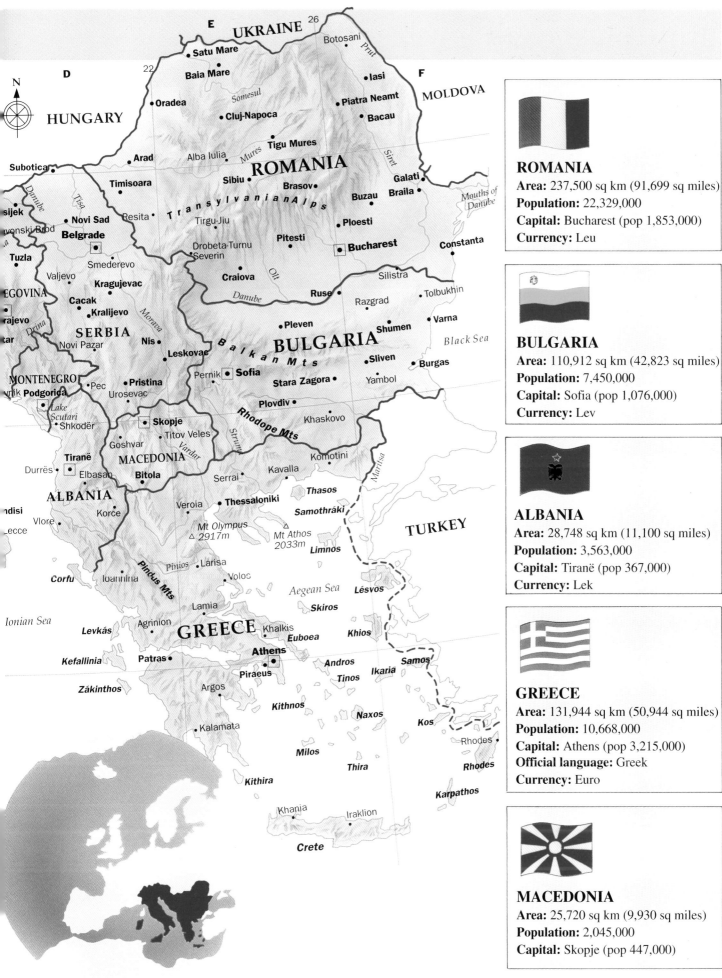

Map Labels

UKRAINE

HUNGARY

MOLDOVA

Satu Mare
Baia Mare
Botosani
Iasi
Oradea
Somesul
Piatra Neamt
Cluj-Napoca
Bacau
Arad
Alba Iulia
Mures
Tigu Mures
Sibiu
ROMANIA
Galati
Timisoara
Brasov
Buzau
Braila
Subotica
Resita
Tirgu-Jiu
Ploesti
Mouths of Danube
Danube
Tisa
Novi Sad
Belgrade
Drobeta-Turnu Severin
Pitesti
Bucharest
Constanta
Tuzla
Smederevo
Craiova
Olt
Silistra
Valjevo
Kragujevac
Danube
Ruse
Razgrad
Tolbukhin
EGOVINA
Cacak
Kralijevo
Morava
Pleven
Shumen
Varna
rajevo
Drina
SERBIA
Nis
Leskovac
Balkan Mts
BULGARIA
Sliven
Burgas
Black Sea
tar
Novi Pazar
Pernik
Sofia
Stara Zagora
Yambol
MONTENEGRO
Pec
Pristina
Urosevac
Plovdiv
Khaskovo
rnik
Podgorica
Lake Scutari
Skopje
Titov Veles
Rhodope Mts
Shkoder
Goshvar
Vardar
Strimn
Komotini
Tirane
MACEDONIA
Kavalla
Marisa
Durres
Elbasan
Bitola
Serrai
ALBANIA
Veroia
Thessaloniki
Thasos
Samothraki
ndisi
Korce
Mt Olympus 2917m
Mt Athos 2033m
ecce
Limnos
Vlore
Pinios
Larisa
Volos
Corfu
Ioannina
Aegean Sea
Lesvos
Skiros
Lamia
Ionian Sea
Levkas
Agrinion
GREECE
Khalkis
Euboea
Khios
Kefallinia
Patras
Athens
Andros
Samos
Zakinthos
Piraeus
Tinos
Ikaria
Argos
Kithnos
Kos
Kalamata
Naxos
Rhodes
Milos
Thira
Rhodes
Kithira
Karpathos
Khania
Iraklion
Crete

Country Data Panels

ROMANIA
Area: 237,500 sq km (91,699 sq miles)
Population: 22,329,000
Capital: Bucharest (pop 1,853,000)
Currency: Leu

BULGARIA
Area: 110,912 sq km (42,823 sq miles)
Population: 7,450,000
Capital: Sofia (pop 1,076,000)
Currency: Lev

ALBANIA
Area: 28,748 sq km (11,100 sq miles)
Population: 3,563,000
Capital: Tiranë (pop 367,000)
Currency: Lek

GREECE
Area: 131,944 sq km (50,944 sq miles)
Population: 10,668,000
Capital: Athens (pop 3,215,000)
Official language: Greek
Currency: Euro

MACEDONIA
Area: 25,720 sq km (9,930 sq miles)
Population: 2,045,000
Capital: Skopje (pop 447,000)

Russia and its Neighbours

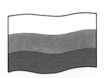

RUSSIAN FEDERATION (RUSSIA)

Area: 17,075,400 sq km (6,592,849 sq miles), the world's largest country

Highest point:
Mount Elbrus 5,633m (18,481ft)

Population: 143,420,000

Capital: Moscow (pop 10,469,000)

Other cities:
St Petersburg (5,214,000)
Nizhny Novgorod (1,331,000)
Novosibirsk (1,426,000)
Yekaterinburg (1,280,000)
Samara (1,260,000)

Official language: Russian

Religions: Christianity, Judaism, Islam

Main products: *Agriculture:* cotton, flax, potatoes, sugar, wheat, cattle, pigs, sheep; *Mining:* coal, copper, gold, iron ore, oil and natural gas; *Industry:* iron and steel, chemicals, machinery, paper, plastics

Currency: Rouble

Government: Federal republic

ESTONIA
Area: 45,100 sq km (17,413 sq miles)
Population: 1,333,000
Capital: Tallinn (pop 391,000)

LATVIA
Area: 64,500 sq km (24,904 sq miles)
Population: 2,290,000
Capital: Riga (pop 733,000)

LITHUANIA
Area: 65,200 sq km (25,174 sq miles)
Population: 3,597,000
Capital: Vilnius (pop 549,000)

BELARUS
Area: 207,600 sq km (80,155 sq miles)
Population: 10,300,000
Capital: Minsk (pop 1,705,000)

UKRAINE
Area: 603,700 sq km (233,090 sq miles)
Population: 46,997,000
Capital: Kyyiv (pop 2,618,000)

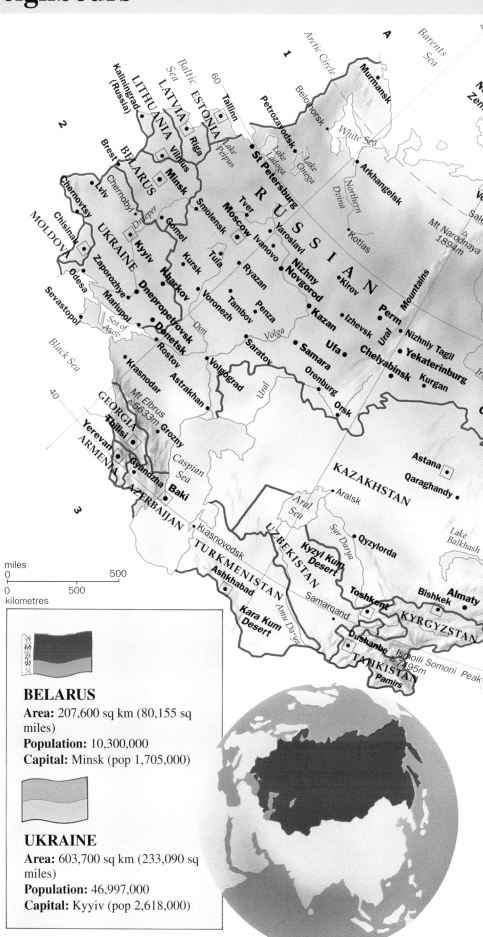

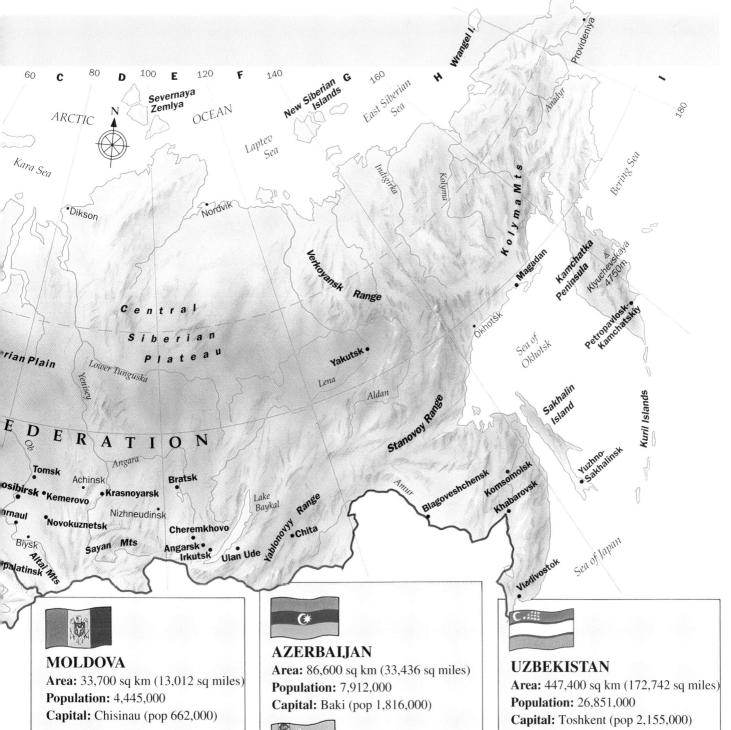

60 **C** 80 **D** 100 **E** 120 **F** 140 160 **G** **H** 180 **I**

ARCTIC **N** Severnaya Zemlya OCEAN

New Siberian Islands

East Siberian Sea

Wrangel I.

Providerniya

Kara Sea

Laptev Sea

Anadyr

•Dikson

Nordvik

Indigirka

Kolyma

Verkoyansk Range

Kolyma Mts

Kamchatka Peninsula

Magadan

Klyuchevskaya △ 4750m

Bering Sea

Central Siberian Plateau

Lower Tunguska

Yenisey

Okhotsk

Sea of Okhotsk

Petropavlosk-Kamchatskiy

rian Plain

Yakutsk•

Lena

Aldan

Sakhalin Island

Kuril Islands

E D E R A T I O N

Ob

Angara

Stanovoy Range

Amur

•Tomsk

Achinsk

Bratsk

Blagoveshchensk

Komsomolsk

osibirsk •Kemerovo **Krasnoyarsk**

Lake Baykal

Yablonovyy Range

Khabarovsk

arnaul

Nizhneudinsk

•Chita

Yuzhno-Sakhalinsk

•Novokuznetsk

Cheremkhovo

Biysk

Sayan Mts

Angarsk•

Altai Mts

Irkutsk

Ulan Ude

Sea of Japan

palatinsk Mts

Vladivostok•

MOLDOVA
Area: 33,700 sq km (13,012 sq miles)
Population: 4,445,000
Capital: Chisinau (pop 662,000)

GEORGIA
Area: 69,700 sq km (26,911 sq miles)
Population: 4,677,000
Capital: Tbilisi (pop 1,064,000)

ARMENIA
Area: 29,800 sq km (11,506 sq miles)
Population: 2,983,000
Capital: Yerevan (pop 1,079,000)

AZERBAIJAN
Area: 86,600 sq km (33,436 sq miles)
Population: 7,912,000
Capital: Baki (pop 1,816,000)

TURKMENISTAN
Area: 488,100 sq km (188,456 sq miles)
Population: 4,952,000
Capital: Ashkhabad (pop 574,000)

KAZAKHSTAN
Area: 2,717,300 sq km (1,049,156 sq miles)
Population: 15,186,000
Capital: Astana (pop 332,000)

UZBEKISTAN
Area: 447,400 sq km (172,742 sq miles)
Population: 26,851,000
Capital: Toshkent (pop 2,155,000)

KYRGYZSTAN
Area: 198,500 sq km (76,641 sq miles)
Population: 5,146,000
Capital: Bishkek (pop 806,000)

TAJIKISTAN
Area: 143,100 sq km (55,251 sq miles)
Population: 7,164,000
Capital: Dushanbe (pop 554,000)

Asia

Asia is the largest continent. As well as China, Japan and India, it contains the major part of the Russian Federation, along with several other countries that were formerly part of the Soviet Union. They include Armenia, Azerbaijan and Georgia, which lie south of the Caucasus Mountains. The other countries are Kazakhstan, Kyrgyzstan, Tajikistan, Turkmenistan and Uzbekistan. These countries lie between the Caspian Sea in the west and China in the east.

China's Chang Jiang (formerly called the Yangtze Kiang) is the longest river. Mount Everest, on Nepal's border with China, is Asia's highest peak.

Asia has more than 3,900 million people, including the Asian part of Russia. It includes the world's two most populous countries, China and India, both with over a billion people.

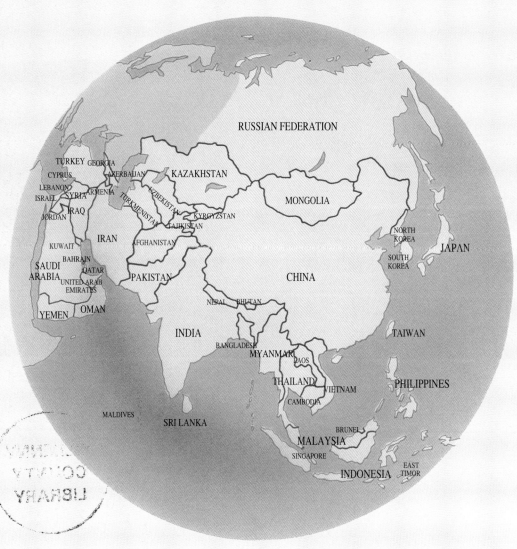

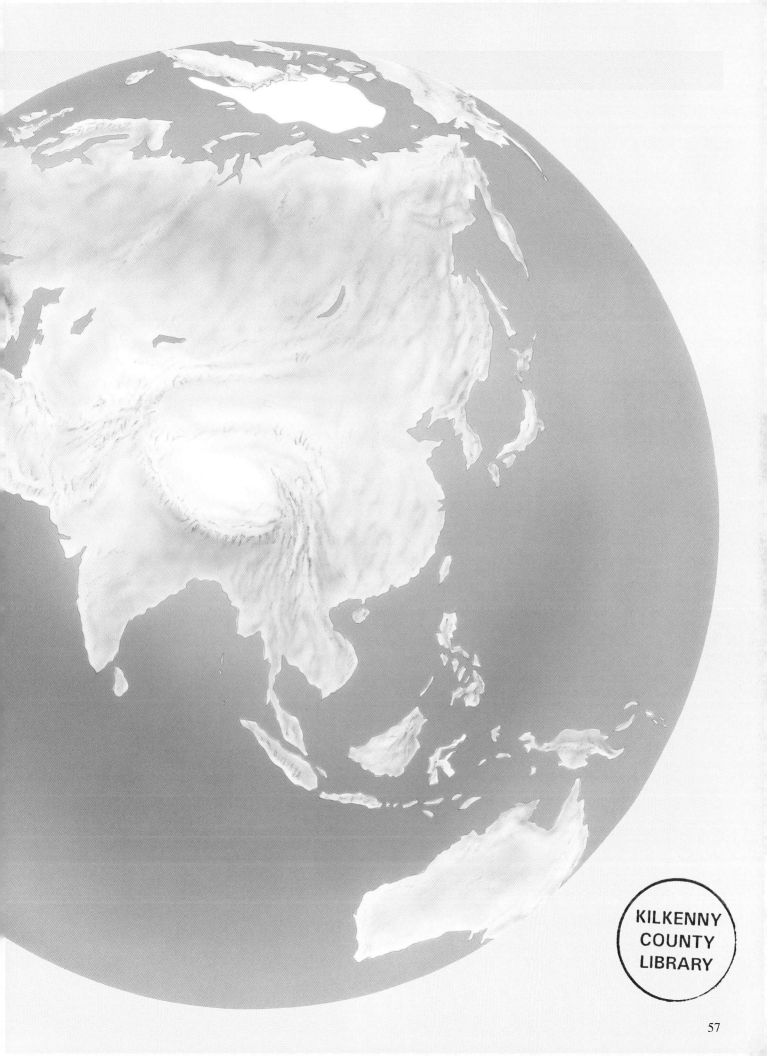

57

Near East

CYPRUS

Area: 9,251 sq km (3,572 sq miles)
Population: 780,000
Capital and largest city: Nicosia
(pop 205,000)

ISRAEL

Area: 20,770 sq km (8,019 sq miles)
Population: 6,277,000
Capital and largest city: Jerusalem
(pop 686,000)
Other large cities:
Tel Aviv-Yafo (2,752,000)
Haifa (865,000)
Holon (164,000)
Official languages: Hebrew, Arabic
Religions: Judaism (79.2%), Islam
(14.9%), Christianity (2.1%), other
including Druze (3.8%)
Currency: Shekel

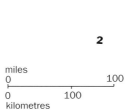

TURKEY

Area: 780,576 sq km (301,382 sq miles)
Population: 69,661,000
Capital: Ankara (pop 3,428,000)
Other large cities:
Istanbul (8,744,000)
Izmir (2,216,000)
Bursa (1,066,000)
Adana (1,041,000)
Official language: Turkish
Religion: Islam (99.2%)
Currency: Turkish Lira

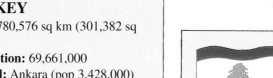

A • Edirne 28 **B**

GREECE

1 Tekirdag **Istanbul** • Üsküdar Bosporus

Sea of
Marmara **Izmit**

Gokceada I. Dardanelles **Adap**

40 • Çanakkale • **Bursa** Sakarya

.:. Troy

• Edremit • Balikesir **Eskisehir**

• Kütahya

• Bergama

N Manisa **2**

• **Izmir** Gediz • Usak

Aegean Sea A•

Lake
Egridir

Aydin Menderes

miles
0 ———————— 100
0 ———— 100
kilometres • **Denizli** **Ispa**

An•

36

• Finike

LEBANON

Area: 10,400 sq km (4,015 sq miles)
Population: 3,826,000
Capital and largest city: Beirut
(pop 1,792,000)
Currency: Lebanese Pound

3

JORDAN

Area: 97,740 sq km (37,738 sq miles)
Population: 5,760,000
Capital and largest city: Amman
(pop 1,237,000)
Currency: Jordanian Dinar

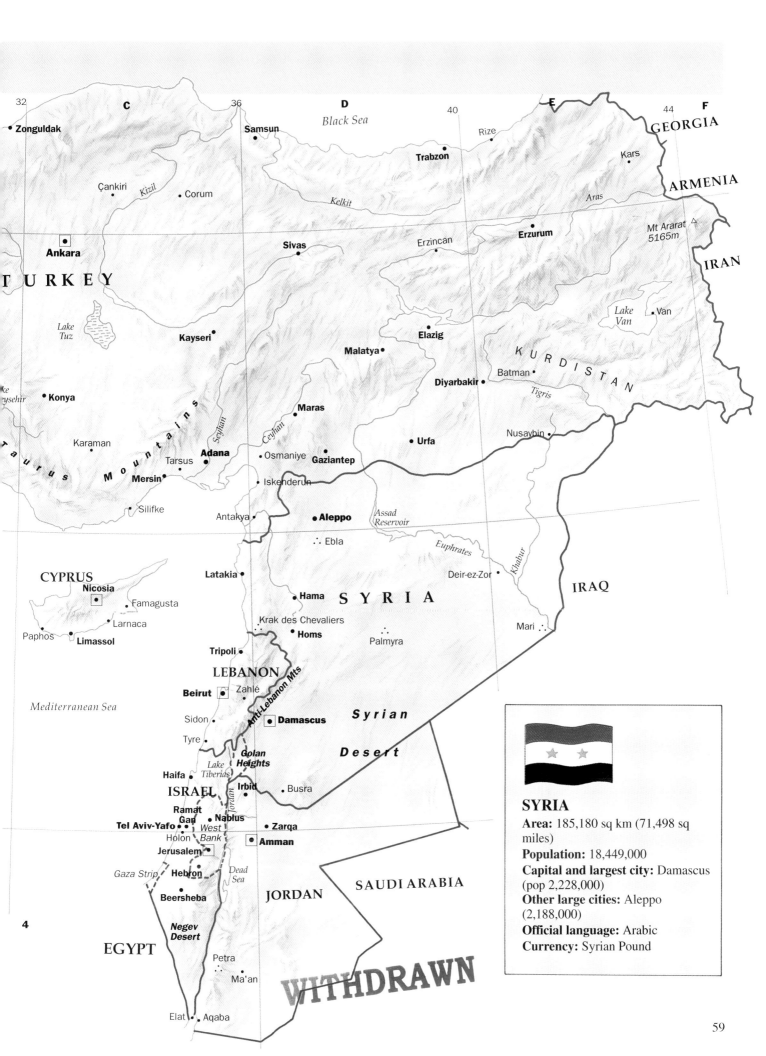

32   C   36   D   40   E   44   F

Zonguldak ●

Black Sea

Samsun ●

GEORGIA

Rize ●

Çankiri ●   *Kizil*   ● Corum   **Trabzon** ●

Kars ●

Kelkit   *Aras*

ARMENIA

● **Ankara**

Sivas ●   Erzincan ●   **Erzurum** ●

Mt Ararat △
5165m

T U R K E Y

IRAN

Lake Tuz

Kayseri ●   **Elazig** ●

Lake Van   ● Van

K U R D I S T A N

Maras ●   **Diyarbakir** ●   Batman ●

Tigris

Konya ●

ysehir   Karaman ●   **Adana** ●   **Maras** ●   ● Osmaniye   **Urfa** ●   Nusaybin ●

aurus   *Mountains*   Tarsus ●   **Gaziantep** ●

Mersin ●

● Silifke   Iskenderun ●

Antakya ●   ● **Aleppo**   *Assad Reservoir*

Euphrates

CYPRUS
Nicosia ⊡   ∴ Ebla   *Khabur*

● Famagusta   Latakia ●   Deir-ez-Zor ●

Paphos ●   Larnaca ●   **S Y R I A**   IRAQ

Limassol ●   **Hama** ●

Krak des Chevaliers ●   ∴ Palmyra   Mari ∴

Homs ●

Tripoli ●

LEBANON   *Anti-Lebanon Mts*

Beirut ⊡   Zahlé ●   *S y r i a n*

Mediterranean Sea   Sidon ●   ⊡ **Damascus**

Tyre ●   *D e s e r t*

Golan Heights

Haifa ●   *Lake Tiberias*   **Irbid** ●   ● Busra

Jordan

ISRAEL

Ramat Gan ●   **Nablus** ●   ● **Zarqa**

Tel Aviv-Yafo ●   *West Bank*

Holon ●   ⊡ **Amman**

Jerusalem ⊡

Gaza Strip   **Hebron** ●   *Dead Sea*

4   **Beersheba** ●   **JORDAN**   **SAUDI ARABIA**

Negev Desert

EGYPT

Petra ∴

Ma'an ●

Elat ●   ● Aqaba

WITHDRAWN

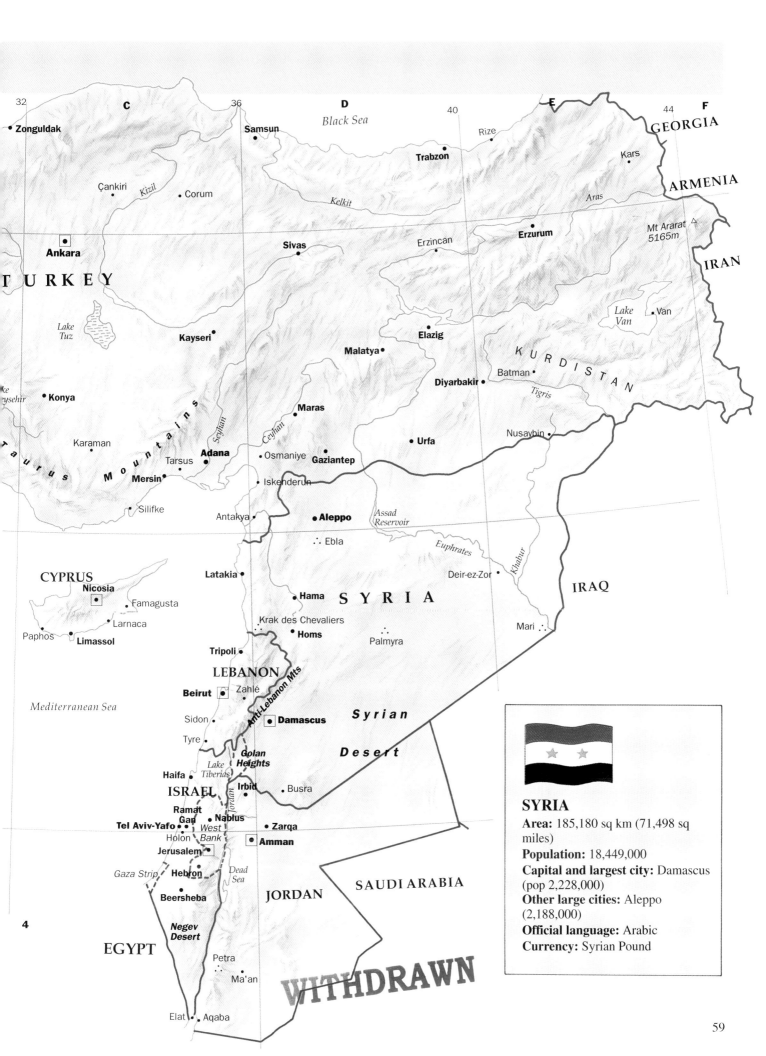

SYRIA

Area: 185,180 sq km (71,498 sq miles)
Population: 18,449,000
Capital and largest city: Damascus (pop 2,228,000)
Other large cities: Aleppo (2,188,000)
Official language: Arabic
Currency: Syrian Pound

Arabian Peninsula and Gulf States

IRAQ

Area: 434,924 sq km (176,925 sq miles)

Population: 26,075,000

Capital and largest city: Baghdad (pop 5,620,000)

Other large cities:
Irbil (2,369,000)

Official language: Arabic

Currency: Iraqi Dinar

SAUDI ARABIA

Area: 2,149,690 sq km (830,000 sq miles)

Population: 26,418,000

Capital: Riyadh (pop 5,126,000)

Other large cities:
Jiddah (3,171,000)

Official language: Arabic

Currency: Saudi Riyal

A · 40 · B · 45 · C · 50

TURKEY

Khvoy · Tabriz · Ardabil · Caspian S

Orumiyeh · Lake Urmia · Rasht

Kurdistan · Zanjan · Elburz

Mosul · Qazvin · Demavend 5604m

Irbil · Tehran

SYRIA · As Sulaymaniyah

Kirkuk

Euphrates · Tigris · Bakhtaran · Hamadan · Qom

I R A Q · Borujerd · Arak

Ar Ramadi · Baghdad · Khorramabad · Kash

Syrian Desert · Zagros · Esf

Karbala · Al Hilah · Dezful

JORDAN · An Najaf · Al Amarah · Shushtar · Mountains

An Nasiriyah · Ahvaz

Ur · Khorramshahr

Basra · Abadan

Al Jawf · **KUWAIT** · S

Tabuk · Kuwait · Bus

An Nafud · Hafar · *The Gu*

Hail

Buraydah · Al Qatif · Damman

Al Wajh · Dhahran · Al Mar

Hejaz · **BAHRAIN**

Al Hufuf · QAT

Medina · Riyadh · Haradh

Yanbu · *Tropic of Cancer*

Red Sea · **S A U D I**

Jiddah · Mecca · **A R A B I A**

At Taif

Rub al Khal

Abha

Jizan · *Hadhramaut*

Farasan Is.

3760m · Sana · **YEMEN**

Al Hudaydah · Mukhalla

Zabid

Mocha · Taiz · Shuqra

Aden

TURKMENISTAN

Gorgan

Neyshabur • **Mashhad**

asht-e Kavir

D a s h t - e L u t

Birjand

• Yazd

R A N

• Kerman

Zahedan

• Bam

AFGHANISTAN

Bandar Abbas

Strait of Hormuz

Chah Bahar

PAKISTAN

Sharjah
Dubai

habi

Gulf of Oman

TED
RAB EMIRATES

Al Khaburah

△ Muscat

3035m

OMAN

Al Masira

h u f a r

Salalah

Kuria Muria I.

Arabian Sea

miles
0 _____ 200
0 _____ 200
kilometres

IRAN
Area: 1,648,000 sq km (636,296 sq miles)
Population: 68,018,000
Capital and largest city: Tehran (pop 7,190,000)
Other large cities:
Mashad (1,990,000)
Esfahan (1,381,000)
Official language: Farsi (Persian)
Currency: Iranian Rial

KUWAIT
Area: 17,818 sq km (6,880 sq miles)
Population: 2,336,000
Capital: Kuwait (pop 1,222,000)
Currency: Kuwaiti Dinar

YEMEN
Area: 527,968 sq km (203,850 sq miles)
Population: 20,727,000
Capital and largest city: Sana (pop 1,469,000)
Other large cities: Aden (562,000)
Currency: Yemen Rial

BAHRAIN
Area: 622 sq km (240 sq miles)
Population: 688,000
Capital: Al Manamah (pop 139,000)

QATAR
Area: 11,000 sq km (4,247 sq miles)
Population: 863,000
Capital and largest city: Doha (pop 286,000)

UNITED ARAB EMIRATES
Area: 83,600 sq km (32,278 sq miles)
Population: 2,563,000
Capital: Abu Dhabi (pop 475,000)

OMAN
Area: 212,457 sq km (82,030 sq miles)
Population: 3,002,000
Capital and largest city: Muscat (pop 638,000)
Religions: Islam (86%), Hinduism (13%)
Currency: Omani Rial

India and Southern Asia

INDIA

Area: 3,287,590 sq km (1,269,346 sq miles)

Highest point: Kanchenjunga, on border with Nepal, 8,598m (28,208ft)

Population: 1,080,264,000

Capital: New Delhi (pop 301,000)

Other large cities:
Mumbai (16,086,000)
Kolkata (13,058,000)
Delhi (12,441,000)
Chennai (6,353,000)
Bangalore (5,567,000)
Hyderabad (5,445,000)

Official languages: Hindi, English

Religions: Hinduism (82.6%), Islam (11.4%), Christianity (2.4%), Sikhism (2%), other religions (1.6%)

Economy: *Services; Agriculture:* rice and other grains, pulses, cotton, sugar cane; *Fishing; Mining:* coal, iron ore, manganese; *Industry:* textiles, food products, steel, machinery, transport equipment

Currency: Indian Rupee

Government: Federal republic

AFGHANISTAN

Area: 647,497 sq km (250,000 sq miles)

Population: 29,929,000

Capital and largest city: Kabul (pop 2,956,000)

Religion: Islam (99%)

Currency: Afghani

PAKISTAN

Area: 796,095 sq km (307,374 sq miles)

Population: 162,420,000

Capital: Islamabad (pop 698,000)

Other large cities:
Karachi (10,032,000)
Lahore (5,452,000)

Official language: Urdu

Religion: Islam (96.7%)

Main products: Rice, cotton, textiles

Currency: Pakistan Rupee

NEPAL

Area: 140,797 sq km (54,362 sq miles)

Highest point: Mount Everest, on the border with China, 8,848m (29,028ft)

Population: 27,677,000

Capital and largest city: Katmandu (pop 741,000)

Official language: Nepali

Currency: Nepali Rupee

(Map of India and Southern Asia)

TURKMENISTAN
Mazar-i-Sharif
Qor
Baghlan
Hindu Kush
Herat
Kabul
Jal
Ghazni
Farah
AFGHANISTAN
IRAN
Kandahar
Rigestan Desert
Quetta
Kalat
PAKISTAN
Sulaiman
Baluchistan Plateau
Sukkur
Indus
D
Gwadar
Nawabshah
Hyderabad
Karachi
Tropic of Cancer
Jamnagar
Raj
Bhavi
Arabian Sea
INDI

C 75

Chitral
Gilgit
The ownership of this area is disputed

Karakoram Range

D 80

K2 8611m

△ Janga Parbat 8126m

Pass
Mardan
ar · Islamabad
· Srinagar
· Leh

Rawalpindi
· Jammu
Gujranwala
odha
· Amritsar
alabad
Lahore · Jullundur
· Ludhiana
Patiala · Chandigarh
Saharanpur · Dehra Dun

H I M A L A Y A

95

BHUTAN
Area: 47,000 sq km (18,147 sq miles)
Population: 2,232,000
Capital: Thimphu (pop 35,000)

E 85 F 90 G

Silgarhi

C H N I A

NEPAL

Meerut
Delhi ·
· Moradabad
· Bikaner
New Delhi · Bareilly
Alwar · Aligarh
Ajmer Jaipur Agra
pur
Gwalior Kanpur
Kota · Jhansi

△ Annapurna 8078m
· Pokhara

Everest 8848m △
Kanchenjunga 8598m △

· Thimphu
BHUTAN

Brahmaputra

Ganges

Lucknow
· Gorakhpur
Faizabad
Allahabad
· Varanasi

· Patna
Bhagalpur
Saidpur
· Guwahati

· Imphal

Gaya
· Dhanbad
Asansol
· Rajshahi
Dhaka ·

BANGLADESH

MYANMAR

adabad
Bhopal · Sagar
· Ujjain
· Indore
Narmada · Jabalpur

Ranchi
Jamshedpur
Howrah
Kolkata (Calcutta)

· Narayangani

Khulna
· Chittagong

Burhanpur
Nagpur
Amravati ·
· Raipur
· Bilaspur

· Cuttack

I N D I A

ik
· Aurangabad
bai
bay)
Godavari
Pune

· Berhampur

Bay of Bengal

miles
0   200
0   200
kilometres

Sholapur
Warangal
hapur
Deccan · Hyderabad
Krishna
Belgaum
Plateau · Vijayawada
Hubli
Guntur

· Vishakhapatnam
· Rajahmundry

Eastern Ghats

· Davangere

alore
Bangalore
· Mysore
· Chennai (Madras)

Calicut
Salem
Coimbatore · Tiruchchirappalli
Cochin
Madurai · Jaffna
Tirunelveli
Trivandrum
Gulf of Mannar
· Trincomalee

SRI LANKA
Area: 65,610 sq km (25,332 sq miles)
Population: 20,065,000
Capital and largest city: Colombo (pop 648,000)
Official languages: Sinhalese, Tamil
Currency: Sri Lankan Rupee

BANGLADESH
Area: 143,998 sq km (55,598 sq miles)
Population: 144,320,000
Capital and largest city: Dhaka (pop 11,560,000)
Other large cities: Chittagong (3,271,000)
Official language: Bengali
Religions: Islam (86.6%), Hinduism (12.1%)
Currency: Taka

N

· Kandy
Colombo ·
Galle

63

China, Japan and the Far East

1

A   84   B   96   C   108

KAZAKHSTAN

44

KYRGYZSTAN

N

Lake Uvs

Lake Hovsgol

Darhan

Erdenet

Ulan Bator

MONGOLIA

TAJIKISTAN

2

• Yining

Tian Shan

• Urumqi

Altai Mts

• Kashi

PAKISTAN

• Shache

Taklimakan Desert

Altun Mts

Gobi Desert

• Yumen

Qilian Mountains

Mu Us Desert

Ba

Kunlun Mountains

Yinchuan

Lake Qinghai

• Xining

Huang He   Great Wall of

• Lanzhou

32

Tibetan Plateau

Baoji   Xi'ar

INDIA

C   H   I   N   A

NEPAL

Himalayas

Xigaze

Everest △ 8848m

• Lhasa

Salween

Chengdu   Nanchong   Yangtze River

Chang Jiang (Yangtze River)

Zigong •   • Chongqing

Luzhou

Zunyi

BHUTAN

Mekong

Giuyang

Shao

• Kunming

Gu

Yunnan Plateau

Luiz

Gejiu

Xi Jiang

MYANMAR   LAOS   VIETNAM

20

W

• Nannin

Zhanjiang

4

Ha

Hain

CHINA

Area: 9,596,961 sq km (3,705,408) sq miles)

Highest point: Mount Everest, on the border with Nepal, 8,848m (29,028ft)

Longest river: Chang Jiang (formerly Yangtze Kiang), 5,530km (3,436 miles)

Population: 1,306,314,000

Capital: Beijing (pop 10,848,000)

Other large cities:
Shanghai (12,887,000)
Tianjin (9,156,000)
Shenyang (4,828,000)
Chongqing (4,635,000)

Official language: Mandarin Chinese

Religions: Confucianism, Buddhism, Taoism, Islam

Economy: *Agriculture:* rice, wheat, oilseed, cotton; *Fishing:* fresh and sea fishing; *Mining:* coal, iron, oil; *Industry:* iron and steel, machinery, textiles; *Services*

Currency: Yuan

Government: People's Republic

MONGOLIA

Area: 1,565,000 sq km (604,250 sq miles)

Population: 2,791,000

Capital and largest city: Ulan Bator (pop 812,000)

Official language: Mongolian

Religions: Tantric Buddhism, Islam

Currency: Tugrik

120

RUSSIA

Lesser Hinggan Range

Greater Hinggan Range

Amur

E

132

F

144

• Qiqihar

• Harbin
Jixi •
Baicheng •
Manchurian Plain
• Mudanjiang
Changchun • • Jilin
Siping •
Shenyang •
Fuxin • • Fushun
• Benxi
Jinzhou • Anshan
Yingkou • Sinuiju
• Beijing
• Tangshan Pyongyang
Tianjin • Nampo
Bo Hai Sea Dalian •
Shijiazhuang Yantai •
uan
• Xingtai Zibo • Weifang
n
Jinan • Qingdao
Anyang
ngzhou
• Kaifeng Lianyungang •
Xuzhou •
yang
Huainan • Nantong •
fan
Nanjing •
Hefei • Wuxi •
Wuhan Suzhou • Shanghai
Wuhu •
ngshi Hangzhou •
Anqing • • Ningbo
• Jingdezhen
Nanchang •
ngsha • Wenzhou
gyang

Chongjin •

Sea of Japan

NORTH KOREA

Hamhung •

Wonsan •

Seoul •

SOUTH KOREA

Inchon •

Taejon •
• Taegu
• Ulsan
Kwangju • Pusan •
Cheju • Hiroshima •

Yellow Sea

East China Sea

Ryukyu Islands

• Fuzhou
Chilung •
Taipei •
Shaoguan • Xiamen •
Shantou • Taichung •
zhou Tainan • TAIWAN
• Hong Kong Gaoxiong •

• Naha

Tropic of Cancer

South China Sea

Asahikawa •

Sapporo • Hokkaido

Hakodate •

Aomori •
• Morioka
Akita •
• Sendai
Niigata •
Honshu JAPAN
• Tokyo
Kanazawa • • Chiba
Kawasaki •
Mt Fuji Yokohama
Kyoto • △3776m
Kobe • Nagoya •
Osaka •
Okayama • Sakai •
Matsuyama •
Shikoku
Kitakyushu •
Fukuoka •
Kumamoto •
Nagasaki •
Kagoshima • Kyushu

PACIFIC OCEAN

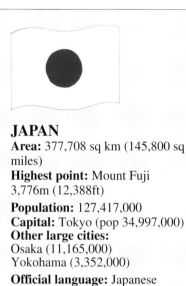

JAPAN
Area: 377,708 sq km (145,800 sq miles)
Highest point: Mount Fuji 3,776m (12,388ft)
Population: 127,417,000
Capital: Tokyo (pop 34,997,000)
Other large cities:
Osaka (11,165,000)
Yokohama (3,352,000)
Official language: Japanese
Religions: Shintoism (39.5%), Buddhism (38.3%)
Main products: Manufactures, including machinery, vehicles, electronic goods, instruments
Currency: Yen
Government: Monarchy

NORTH KOREA
Area: 120,538 sq km (46,540 sq miles)
Population: 22,912,000
Capital and largest city: Pyongyang (pop 3,228,000)

SOUTH KOREA
Area: 98,484 sq km (38,025 sq miles)
Population: 48,641,000
Capital and largest city: Seoul (pop 9,714,000)

TAIWAN
Area: 36,000 sq km (13,900 sq miles)
Population: 22,894,000
Capital and largest city: Taipei (pop 2,550,000)

miles
0   500
0   500
kilometres

South-Eastern Asia

THAILAND
Area: 514,000 sq km (198,457 sq miles)
Population: 64,185,000
Capital and largest city: Bangkok (pop 6,486,000)
Official language: Thai
Currency: Baht

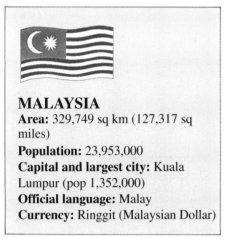

MALAYSIA
Area: 329,749 sq km (127,317 sq miles)
Population: 23,953,000
Capital and largest city: Kuala Lumpur (pop 1,352,000)
Official language: Malay
Currency: Ringgit (Malaysian Dollar)

SINGAPORE
Area: 581 sq km (224 sq miles)
Population: 4,253,000
Capital and largest city: Singapore (pop 4,253,000)
Official languages: Chinese, Malay, Tamil, English
Currency: Singapore Dollar

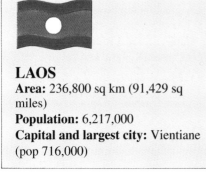

LAOS
Area: 236,800 sq km (91,429 sq miles)
Population: 6,217,000
Capital and largest city: Vientiane (pop 716,000)

MYANMAR (Burma)
Area: 676,552 sq km (261,218 sq miles)
Population: 46,997,000
Capital and largest city: Yangon (formerly Rangoon) pop 3,874,000
Official language: Burmese
Currency: Kyat

INDIA

BANGLADESH

MYANMAR (Burma)

CHINA

Tropic of Cancer

Myitkyina

Mandalay

Akyab

Meiktila

Irrawaddy

Chiang Mai

LAOS

Luang Prabang

Red

Hanoi

VIETNAM

Vinh

Bassein

Pegu

Yangon

Vientiane

Phitsanulok

Udon Thani

THAILAND

Mekong

Annam

Moulmein

Nakhon Sawan

Khon Kaen

Ubon Ratchathani

Pakse

Da Na

Bangkok

Nakhon Ratchasima

Sisophon

Chon Buri

Batambang

Lake Tonle Sap

CAMBODIA

Kratie

Da L

Mergui

Phnom Penh

Ho Chi Minh

Rach Gia

My Th

Can Tho

Nakhon Si Thammarat

Phuket

Andaman Sea

Hat Yai

Songkhla

Banda Aceh

Kota Baharu

INDIAN OCEAN

George Town

M A L A

Ipoh

Medan

Pematangsiantar

Simeulue

Lake Toba

Kelang

Kuala Lumpur

Nias

Sumatra

Johor Baharu

Singapore

Pakanbaru

Padang

Pontia

Siberut

Kerintji 3805m

Jambi

Bangka

I N D O

Barisan Range

Palembang

Be

Mentawai Islands

Tanjungkarang

Jakarta

Bogor

Ban

Sukabumi

Peka

Equator

Gulf of Thailand

miles
0 — 500
0 — 500
kilometres

VIETNAM
Area: 329,556 sq km (127,242 sq miles)
Population: 83,536,000
Capital city: Hanoi (pop 3,977,000)
Currency: Dong

BRUNEI
Area: 5,765 sq km (2,226 sq miles)
Population: 372,000
Capital and largest city: Bandar Seri Begawan (pop 61,000)

CAMBODIA
Area: 181,035 sq km (69,898 sq miles)
Population: 13,636,000
Capital and largest city: Phnom Penh (pop 1,157,000)
Currency: Riel

PHILIPPINES
Area: 300,000 sq km (115,831 sq miles)
Population: 87,857,000
Capital and largest city: Manila (pop 10,352,000)
Currency: Philippine Peso

INDONESIA
Area: 1,889,960 sq km (729,718 sq miles)
Population: 241,974,000
Capital and largest city: Jakarta (pop 12,296,000)
Currency: Rupiah

EAST TIMOR
Area: 14,609 sq km (5,641 sq miles)
Population: 1,041,000
Capital: Dili (pop 49,000)

.10°

C 120° D

130° E

140° F

South China Sea

Ranh

Luzon

Aparri
Baguio
San Carlos
Caloocan
Manila
Lucena
Batangas
Mindoro

PHILIPPINES

△ *Mayon Volcano 2421m*
Samar

Panay
Iloilo
Bacolod
Cadiz
Cebu
Leyte
Negros
Bohol

Palawan

Sulu Sea

Butuan
Iligan
Cagayan de Oro
Mindanao
Zamboanga
Basilan
Mt Apo △ 2954m
Davao
General Santos

PACIFIC OCEAN

ndar Seri Begawan
BRUNEI

Sabah

Tawau

Celebes Sea

Talaud Is.

Sangihe Is.

Manado

Halmahera

Waigeo

Manokwari

Sarmi

intang

Borneo

Samarinda
Palu
Balikpapan

Sulawesi (Celebes)

Obi *Misool*

Sula Is. *Ceram Sea*

Ceram Fakfak

New Guinea
Maoke △ *Range*
Puncak Jaya 5030m

West Papua

E S I A

Banjarmasin
Majene
Kendari

Buru
Ambon

PAPUA NEW GUINEA

Java Sea

Ujung Pandang

Banda Sea

Aru Is.

arang

Flores Sea

akarta
Surabaya
Malang *Bali*
akarta

Lombok *Sumbawa* *Flores*

Sumba

Wetar

Tanimbar Is.

Dili EAST TIMOR

Timor

Merauke

Sarawak
ing

a l i m a n t a n

Africa

Africa is the world's second largest continent. Much of the land is wilderness. Areas with few people include the Sahara in North Africa, the world's biggest desert, and the Kalahari and Namib deserts in southern Africa. Africa has dense forests around the Equator, together with huge grasslands, the home of many wild animals.

The continent's rivers include the world's longest, the Nile. The highest mountain is Kilimanjaro, an old volcano in Tanzania.

Africa contains 53 independent countries, with a total population of more than 890 million. A few countries are rich in minerals and some have industries, but more than half of the people of Africa are poor farmers.

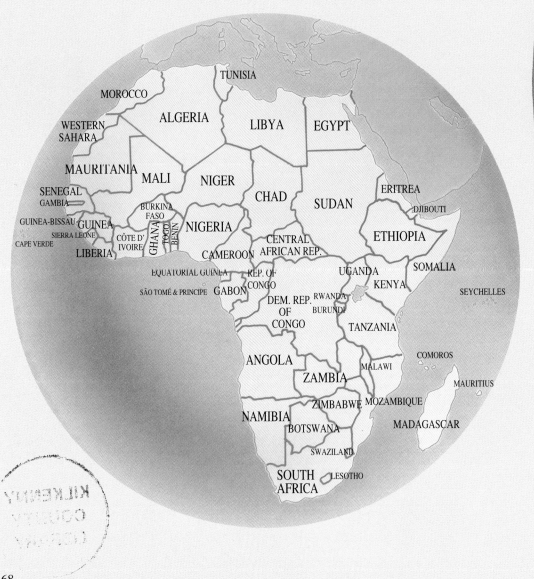

North Africa

ALGERIA
Area: 2,381,741 sq km (919,595 sq miles)
Population: 32,532,000
Capital: Algiers (pop 3,060,000)

TUNISIA
Area: 163,610 sq km (63,170 sq miles)
Population: 10,075,000
Capital: Tunis (pop 1,996,000)

N

MAURITANIA
Area: 1,030,700 sq km (397,956 sq miles)
Population: 3,087,000
Capital: Nouakchott (pop 600,000)

MOROCCO
Area: 446,550 sq km (172,414 sq miles)
Population: 32,726,000
Capital: Rabat (pop 1,759,000)

WESTERN SAHARA
(occupied by Morocco)
Area: 266,000 sq km (102,703 sq miles)
Population: 267,000

MALI
Area: 1,240,000 sq km (478,767 sq miles)
Population: 11,415,000
Capital: Bamako (pop 1,264,000)

NIGER
Area: 1,267,000 sq km (489,191 sq miles)
Population: 12,163,000
Capital: Niamey (pop 890,000)

A   B   C   D

10°   0°   10°

ATLANTIC OCEAN

Algiers   Annaba   Tunis
Tangier   Ceuta (Sp.)   Oran   Blida   Sétif   Constantine   Sousse
Melilla   Sidi-bel-Abbès   Batna   Sfax
Kenitra   Tetouan   (Sp.)   TUNISIA   Tripoli
Rabat   Fez   Oujda   Misurata
Casablanca   Meknès
High Atlas Mts
Safi   Ghardaia
Marrakesh   Béchar
Agadir   Toubkal
4165m
30°   MOROCCO   ALGERIA   LIBYA

Laâyoune   S   a   h   a   r   a

2   WESTERN
SAHARA   Tropic of Cancer   Ahaggar Mts   Tahat
2918m

Nouadhibou   Atar   Air Mts
20°   MAURITANIA   MALI   NIGER
Nouakchott   Timbuktu   s   a   h   e   l
Senegal   Niger   Gao   Agades
3   Mopti   Zinder   Lake Chad
Kayes   Niamey   Maradi
SENEGAL   Bamako   Ségou   N'Djamena
BURKINA
FASO   NIGERIA
GUINEA   BENIN
10°   Mound
CÔTE D'IVOIRE   CAMEROON

70

LIBYA
Area: 1,759,000 sq km (679,362 sq miles)
Population: 5,766,000
Capital: Tripoli (pop 2,006,000)

CHAD
Area: 1,284,000 sq km (495,755 sq miles)
Population: 9,657,000
Capital: N'Djamena (pop 797,000)

EGYPT
Area: 1,001,449 sq km (386,662 sq miles)
Population: 77,506,000
Capital: Cairo (pop 10,834,000)

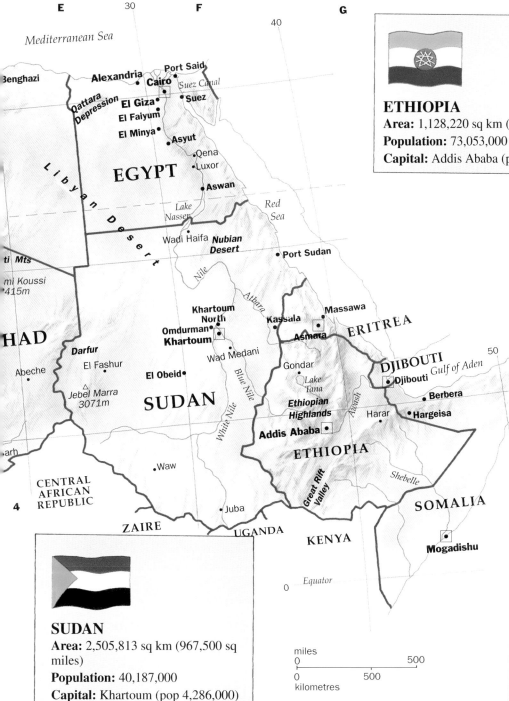

E 30 F 40 G

Mediterranean Sea

Benghazi
Alexandria
Port Said
Cairo
Suez Canal
Qattara Depression
El Giza
Suez
El Faiyum
El Minya
Asyut
Qena
Luxor
EGYPT
Aswan
Libyan Desert
Lake Nassen
Red Sea
ti Mts
mi Koussi 415m
Wadi Haifa
Nubian Desert
Port Sudan
Nile
Atbara
Khartoum North
Massawa
Kassala
Omdurman
Asmara
ERITREA
Khartoum
HAD
Darfur
El Fashur
Wad Medani
Gondar
DJIBOUTI
Gulf of Aden
Abeche
El Obeid
Lake Tana
Djibouti
Berbera
Jebel Marra 3071m
Blue Nile
White Nile
Ethiopian Highlands
Harar
Hargeisa
SUDAN
Addis Ababa
Awash
Shebelle
Waw
ETHIOPIA
CENTRAL AFRICAN REPUBLIC
Great Rift Valley
SOMALIA
4
Juba
ZAIRE
UGANDA
KENYA
Mogadishu
Equator

miles
0   500
0   500
kilometres

ETHIOPIA
Area: 1,128,220 sq km (435,608 sq miles)
Population: 73,053,000
Capital: Addis Ababa (pop 2,723,000)

DJIBOUTI
Area: 22,000 sq km (8,494 sq miles)
Population: 477,000
Capital: Djibouti (pop 502,000)

ERITREA
Area: 93,680 sq km (36,170 sq miles)
Population: 4,670,000
Capital: Asmara (pop 556,000)

SUDAN
Area: 2,505,813 sq km (967,500 sq miles)
Population: 40,187,000
Capital: Khartoum (pop 4,286,000)

SOMALIA
Area: 637,657 sq km (246,201 sq miles)
Population: 8,592,000
Capital: Mogadishu (pop 1,175,000)

West Africa

Cape Verde Islands

Santa Antão
Sal I.
Boa Vista I.
Sào Tiago I.
Praia
Brava

1

16

2

A   21   B

CAPE VERDE
Area: 4,033 sq km (1,557 sq miles)
Population: 418,000
Capital: Praia (pop 107,000)

GAMBIA
Area: 11,295 sq km (4,361 sq miles)
Population: 1,595,000
Capital: Banjul (pop 372,000)

GUINEA-BISSAU
Area: 36,125 sq km (13,948 sq miles)
Population: 1,413,000
Capital: Bissau (pop 336,000)

GUINEA
Area: 245,857 sq km (94,926 sq miles)
Population: 9,453,000
Capital: Conakry (pop 1,366,000)

C   15   D

MAURITANIA

3

St Louis

Senegal

15

Thiès
Dakar
Kaolack

SENEGAL

Banjul

GAMBIA

Gambia

Ziguinchor

4

Bissau

GUINEA-
BISSAU

Bijagos I.

Futa Jalon

Labé

10

E

MALI

Niger

GUINEA

Kindia

Kankan

ATLANTIC
OCEAN

Conakry

10

Makeni

Korhogo

CÔTE
D'IVOIR
(IVORY COA

Freetown

SIERRA
LEONE

5

Bo
Kenema

Mt Nimba
1752m

Boua

Man

Sherbro I.

Bong
Range

Daloa
Yamoussoukr

Monrovia

LIBERIA

Cavally

Gagnoa

Buchanan

Sassandra

5

6

SIERRA LEONE
Area: 71,740 sq km (27,699 sq miles)
Population: 5,867,000
Capital: Freetown (pop 921,000)

LIBERIA
Area: 111,369 sq km (43,000 sq miles)
Population: 2,900,000
Capital: Monrovia (pop 572,000)

SENEGAL
Area: 196,192 sq km (75,750 sq miles)
Population: 11,706,000
Capital: Dakar (pop 2,167,000)

miles
0   200
0   200
kilometres

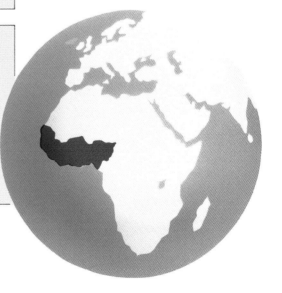

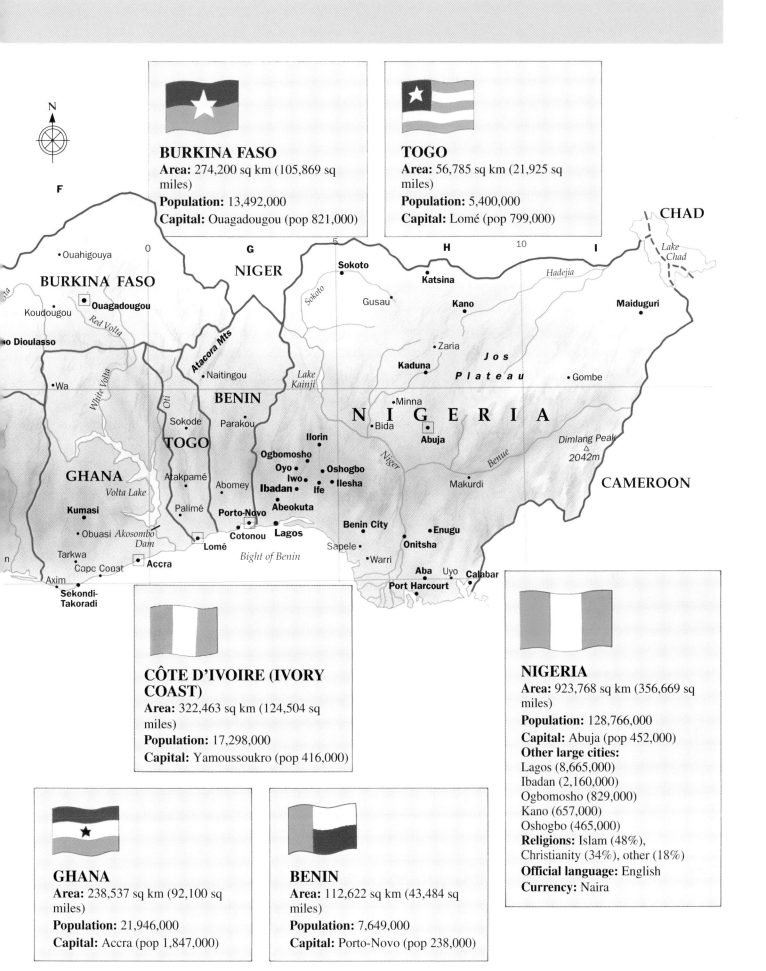

BURKINA FASO
Area: 274,200 sq km (105,869 sq miles)
Population: 13,492,000
Capital: Ouagadougou (pop 821,000)

TOGO
Area: 56,785 sq km (21,925 sq miles)
Population: 5,400,000
Capital: Lomé (pop 799,000)

CÔTE D'IVOIRE (IVORY COAST)
Area: 322,463 sq km (124,504 sq miles)
Population: 17,298,000
Capital: Yamoussoukro (pop 416,000)

NIGERIA
Area: 923,768 sq km (356,669 sq miles)
Population: 128,766,000
Capital: Abuja (pop 452,000)
Other large cities:
Lagos (8,665,000)
Ibadan (2,160,000)
Ogbomosho (829,000)
Kano (657,000)
Oshogbo (465,000)
Religions: Islam (48%), Christianity (34%), other (18%)
Official language: English
Currency: Naira

GHANA
Area: 238,537 sq km (92,100 sq miles)
Population: 21,946,000
Capital: Accra (pop 1,847,000)

BENIN
Area: 112,622 sq km (43,484 sq miles)
Population: 7,649,000
Capital: Porto-Novo (pop 238,000)

Central Africa

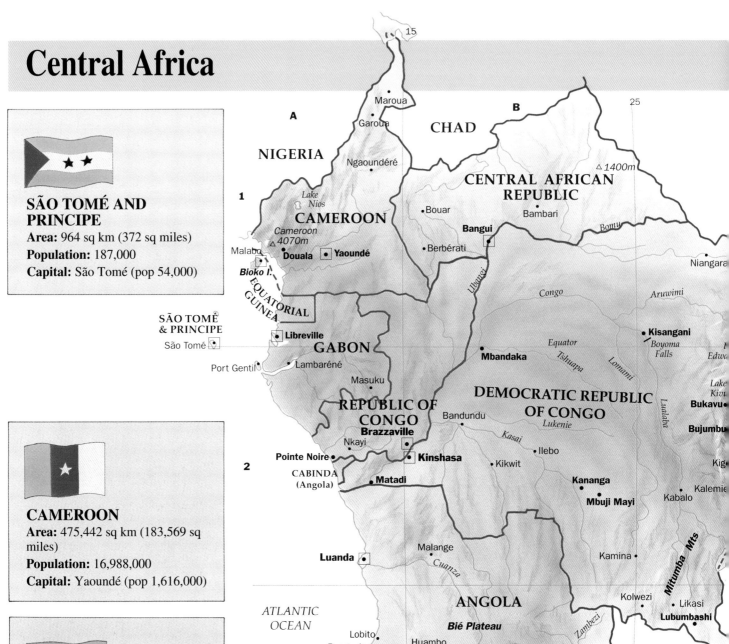

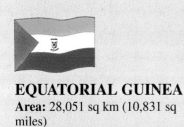

SÃO TOMÉ AND PRINCIPE
Area: 964 sq km (372 sq miles)
Population: 187,000
Capital: São Tomé (pop 54,000)

CAMEROON
Area: 475,442 sq km (183,569 sq miles)
Population: 16,988,000
Capital: Yaoundé (pop 1,616,000)

EQUATORIAL GUINEA
Area: 28,051 sq km (10,831 sq miles)
Population: 529,000
Capital: Malabo (pop 95,000)

GABON
Area: 267,667 sq km (103,347 sq miles)
Population: 1,394,000
Capital: Libreville (pop 611,000)

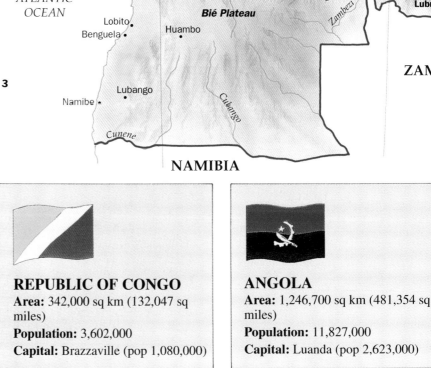

REPUBLIC OF CONGO
Area: 342,000 sq km (132,047 sq miles)
Population: 3,602,000
Capital: Brazzaville (pop 1,080,000)

ANGOLA
Area: 1,246,700 sq km (481,354 sq miles)
Population: 11,827,000
Capital: Luanda (pop 2,623,000)

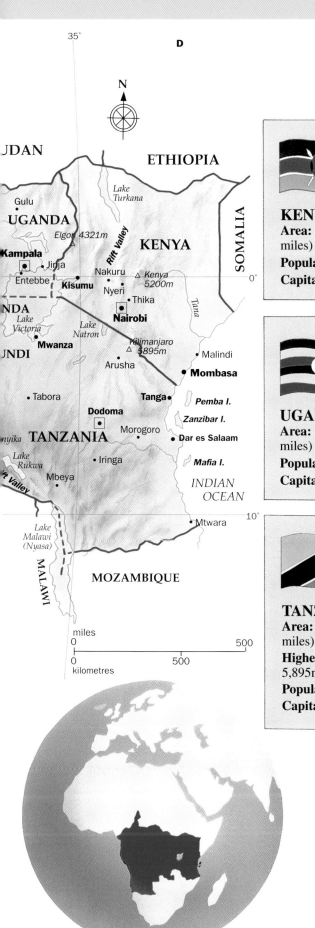

35°

D

N

JDAN

ETHIOPIA

Gulu

Lake
Turkana

UGANDA

Elgon 4321m

KENYA

Kampala

Jinja

Nakuru

Rift Valley

SOMALIA

Entebbe

Kisumu

Nyeri

△ Kenya
5200m

0°

NDA

Thika

Tana

Lake
Victoria

Nairobi

Lake
Natron

JNDI

Mwanza

Kilimanjaro
△ 5895m

Malindi

Arusha

Mombasa

Tabora

Tanga

Pemba I.

Dodoma

Morogoro

Zanzibar I.

nyika

TANZANIA

Dar es Salaam

Lake
Rukwa

Iringa

Mafia I.

INDIAN
OCEAN

Mbeya

Rift Valley

10°

Mtwara

Lake
Malawi
(Nyasa)

MALAWI

MOZAMBIQUE

miles
0   500
0   500
kilometres

KENYA
Area: 582,646 sq km (224,961 sq miles)
Population: 33,830,000
Capital: Nairobi (pop 2,575,000)

UGANDA
Area: 236,036 sq km (91,134 sq miles)
Population: 27,269,000
Capital: Kampala (pop 1,246,000)

TANZANIA
Area: 945,087 sq km (364,900 sq miles)
Highest point: Mount Kilimanjaro 5,895m (19,340ft)
Population: 36,766,000
Capital: Dodoma (pop 155,000)

CENTRAL AFRICAN REPUBLIC
Area: 622,984 sq km (240,535 sq miles)
Population: 4,238,000
Capital: Bangui (pop 698,000)

DEMOCRATIC REPUBLIC OF CONGO
Area: 2,345,409 sq km (905,568 sq miles)
Population: 60,764,000
Capital: Kinshasa (pop 5,277,000)
Official language: French
Currency: Zaire

RWANDA
Area: 26,338 sq km (10,169 sq miles)
Population: 8,441,000
Capital: Kigali (pop 656,000)

BURUNDI
Area: 27,834 sq km (10,747 sq miles)
Population: 7,795,000
Capital: Bujumbura (pop 378,000)

Southern Africa

ZAMBIA
Area: 752,614 sq km (290,586 sq miles)
Population: 11,262,000
Capital: Lusaka (pop 1,394,000)

MALAWI
Area: 118,484 sq km (45,747 sq miles)
Population: 12,707,000
Capital: Lilongwe (pop 587,000)

NAMIBIA
Area: 824,292 sq km (318,261 sq miles)
Population: 2,031,000
Capital: Windhoek (pop 237,000)

B

30°

Lake Tanganyika

Lake Mweru

DEMOCRATIC REPUBLIC OF CONGO

Kasama

Lake Bangweulu

40°

C

TANZANIA

Ruvuma

1

Mufulira

Chingola •

Kitwe • • Ndola

Muchinga Mts

Luangwa

Lake Malawi (Nyasa)

MALAWI

Lichinga

• Per

ZAMBIA

Kabwe •

Lilongwe □

20°

NAMIBIA
Area: 824,292 sq km (318,261 sq miles)
Population: 2,031,000
Capital: Windhoek (pop 237,000)

A

15°

□ **Lusaka**

Kafue

Cabora Bassa Dam

Shire

Nampula • • Moçambic

ANGOLA

Zambezi

Kariba Dam

Tete •

• Blantyre

Livingstone

Lake Kariba

Okavango

Caprivi Strip

Victoria Falls

Harare
□

ZIMBABWE

Mutare •

MOZAMBIQUE

Quelimane

Rundu

Etosha Pan

• Tsumeb

Okavango Basin

Kwekwe •

Gweru •

• Chimoio

Mozambique Channel

2

Namib

NAMIBIA

• Masvingo

△ Mt Binga
2430m

• Beira

Windhoek
□

Orapa •

Francistown •

• **Bulawayo**

Walvis Bay
(S. Africa)

Desert

BOTSWANA

Bobonong •

Beitbridge

Serowe •

K a l a h a r i

Limpopo

Tropic of Capricorn

25°

Mahalapye •

D e s e r t

Lüderitz

Keetmanshoop

Pietersburg •

• Inhambane

• Xai Xai

Gaborone □

□ **Pretoria**

Mafikeng •   **Krugersdorp** □

Johannesburg •   • **Springs**

Upington •

Potchefstroom •

• **Germiston**

Vereeniging

□ **Maputo**

□ Mbabane

SWAZILAND

INDIAN OCEAN

Orange

Vaal

• Kroonstad

• Welkom

• Newcastle

• Ladysmith

Kimberley •

□

Maseru •

• **Pietermaritzburg**
• **Durban**

Bloemfontein

LESOTHO

△ *Thabana Ntlenyana 3482m*

3

ATLANTIC OCEAN

SOUTH   AFRICA

Drakensberg

Beaufort West •

• Queenstown

Great Karroo

Paarl • Worcester

Little Karroo

Uitenhage •

• **East London**

Cape Town □

• Mosselbaai

Port Elizabeth

Cape of Good Hope

miles
0   500

0   500
kilometres

MOZAMBIQUE
Area: 801,590 sq km (309,496 sq miles)
Population: 19,407,000
Capital: Maputo (pop 1,221,000)

D   50°

N

COMOROS
ISLANDS

Antsiranana

Maromokotro △
2876m

Mahajanga

MADAGASCAR

Toamasina

Antananarivo □

Antsirabe

Fianarantasoa

oliara

Faradofay

COMOROS
Area: 2,171 sq km (838 sq miles)
Population: 671,000
Capital: Moroni (pop 53,000)

ZIMBABWE
Area: 390,580 sq km (150,804 sq miles)
Population: 12,161,000
Capital: Harare (pop 1,469,000)

SOUTH AFRICA
Area: 1,221,037 sq km (471,445 sq miles)
Population: 44,344,000
Capital: Pretoria (administrative, 1,209,000), Cape Town (legislative, 2,967,000), Bloemfontein (judicial, 381,000)
Other large cities: Johannesburg (2,732,000) Durban (2,370,000)
Religions: Christianity (78.1%), Hinduism (2.1%), Islam (1.4%), other (18.4%)
Official languages: Afrikaans, English
Currency: Rand

BOTSWANA
Area: 581,730 sq km (224,607 sq miles)
Population: 1,640,000
Capital: Gaborone (pop 199,000)

MADAGASCAR
Area: 587,041 sq km (226,658 sq miles)
Population: 18,040,000
Capital: Antananarivo (pop 1,678,000)

SWAZILAND
Area: 17,363 sq km (6,704 sq miles)
Population: 1,138,000
Capital: Mbabane (pop 70,000)

LESOTHO
Area: 30,355 sq km (11,720 sq miles)
Population: 2,031,000
Capital: Maseru (pop 170,000)

Australia and Oceania

Australia is the only country which is also a continent. It is the smallest of the world's seven continents. Australia is part of a region called Oceania, which also includes New Zealand, Papua New Guinea and many islands of the Pacific Ocean.

The longest river in Australia is the Murray. It flows throughout the year, unlike the slightly longer Darling River, parts of which dry up in winter. Papua New Guinea has the highest mountains in Oceania. New Zealand's highest peak is Mount Cook. Australia's is Mount Kosciusko.

Australia is a mainly dry continent, with only about 20 million people. Most Australians live in a few cities on the coast, including Sydney and Melbourne. The rest of Oceania has about 12 million people.

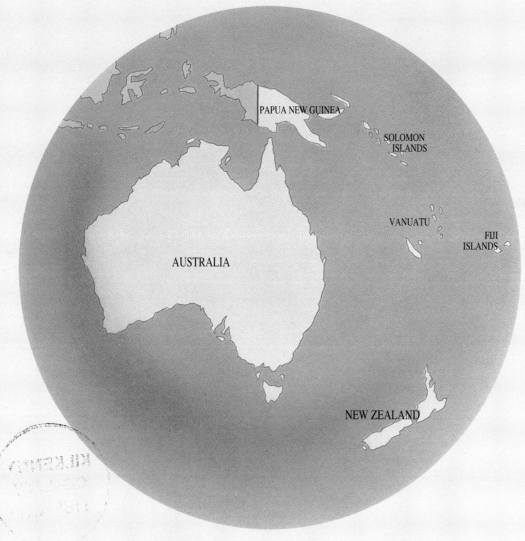

PAPUA NEW GUINEA

SOLOMON
ISLANDS

VANUATU

FIJI
ISLANDS

AUSTRALIA

NEW ZEALAND

130   C   140   D   150

New Ireland

Wewak   *Bismarck Sea*

Rabaul

Sepik

1   Mt Wilhelm   Madang   **New Britain**
4508m △

PAPUA NEW GUINEA   **Bouga**

Lae   *Solomon*

Port Moresby □   Owen Stanley Range

Arafura Sea   *Torres Strait*   **Cape York**

10   **Cape York Peninsula**   *Coral Sea*

B   Melville I.   Cooktown

Timor Sea   · Darwin   **Arnhem Land**   *Gulf of Carpentaria*   Cairns ·   Great

A   INDIAN OCEAN   Wyndham ·   **Kimberley Plateau**   Townsville   Barrier Reef

2   Derby ·   **NORTHERN TERRITORY**   Richmond ·   Mackay ·

Broome ·   Tennant Creek ·   Mount Isa ·   Dividing

Great Sandy Desert   **QUEENSLAND**   Rockhampton ·

20   Dampier ·   · Port Hedland   **A U S T R A L I A**   · Bunda

Macdonnell Range   **Great Artesian Basin**   Maryborough ·

Alice Springs ·   **Simpson Desert**   Great

Gibson Desert   Ayers Rock △   **Musgrave Range**   Range   **Bris**

867m   Carnarvon ·   **WESTERN AUSTRALIA**   Toowoomba ·   Ipswich ·

3   Mount Magnet ·   **Great Victoria Desert**   **SOUTH AUSTRALIA**   *Lake Eyre*   Lis

Musgrave Range   Grafton

Geraldton ·   **Nullarbor Plain**   *Lake Torrens*   Bourke ·   Darling

Kalgoorlie ·   *Lake Gairdner*   Broken Hill ·   **NEW SOUTH WALES**   Maitland ·

30   · Norseman   Woomera ·   Port Augusta   **Newcastle**

Perth   Whyalla ·   Port Pirie ·   Wagga Wagga   **Sydney**

Fremantle ·   Elizabeth ·   Dividing   **Wollongong**

Bunbury ·   *Great Australian Bight*   **Adelaide**   Murray   **Canberra**
AUSTRALIAN CAPITAL TERRIT

Albany ·   **Kangaroo I.**   **VICTORIA**   Albury   △Mt Kosciusko 2230m

4   Bendigo ·   **Great**

Ballarat ·   **Melbourne**

Geelong ·

Bass Strait   **Flinders I.**

King I.

TASMANIA   △ · Launceston
Mt Ossa 1617m

40   5   **Hobart**

miles
0   500
0   500
kilometres

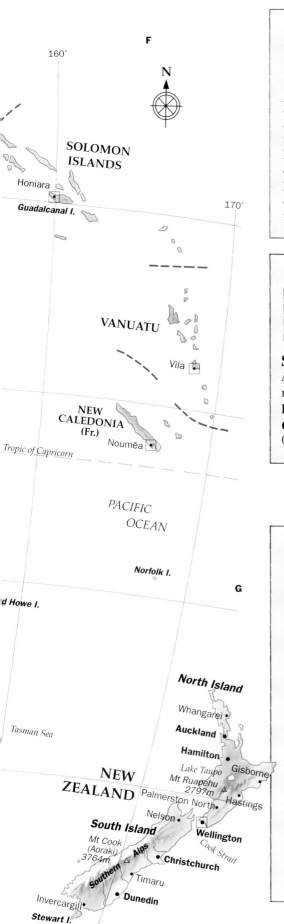

160°

F

N

SOLOMON
ISLANDS

Honiara

Guadalcanal I.

170°

VANUATU

Vila

NEW
CALEDONIA
(Fr.)

Nouméa

Tropic of Capricorn

PACIFIC
OCEAN

Norfolk I.

G

d Howe I.

Tasman Sea

North Island

Whangarei

Auckland

Hamilton

Lake Taupo   Gisborne
Mt Ruapehu
2797m   Hastings
Palmerston North

Nelson

NEW
ZEALAND   Wellington
Cook Strait
South Island
Mt Cook
(Aoraki)   Alps
3764m   Christchurch
Southern
Timaru

Invercargill

Dunedin

Stewart I.

PAPUA NEW GUINEA
Area: 461,691 sq km (178,260 sq miles)
Highest point: Mount Wilhelm 4,508m (14,790ft)
Population: 5,545,000
Capital and largest city: Port Moresby (pop 275,000)

SOLOMON ISLANDS
Area: 28,446 sq km (10,983 sq miles)
Population: 538,000
Capital and largest city: Honiara (pop 56,000)

NEW ZEALAND
Area: 268,676 sq km (103,736 sq miles)
Population: 4,035,000
Capital: Wellington (pop 343,000)
Other large cities: Auckland (1,063,000), Christchurch (331,000)
Official language: English
Religion: Christianity
Economy: *Agriculture:* wool, meat, dairy products; *Mining:* natural gas, iron ore, coal; *Industry:* processed foods, wood and paper, textiles, machinery
Currency: New Zealand Dollar
Government: Constitutional monarchy

VANUATU
Area: 14,763 sq km (5,700 sq miles)
Population: 206,000
Capital: Vila (pop 34,000)

AUSTRALIA
Area: 7,686,848 sq km (2,967,909 sq miles)
Highest point: Mt. Kosciusko 2,230m (7,316ft)
Population: 20,090,000
Capital: Canberra (pop 373,000)
Other large cities: Sydney (4,099,000), Melbourne (3,447,000), Brisbane (1,626,000)
Official language: English
Religion: Christianity
Economy: *Agriculture:* wool, meat, wheat, fruit, sugar; *Mining:* bauxite, coal, iron ore, copper, oil and natural gas, uranium; *Industry:* machinery and transport equipment, processed foods, chemicals, iron and steel, paper, textiles
Currency: Australian Dollar
Government: Constitutional monarchy

NEW CALEDONIA (FRANCE)
Area: 19,058 sq km (7,358 sq miles)
Population: 213,000
Capital: Nouméa (pop 65,000)

Pacific Ocean

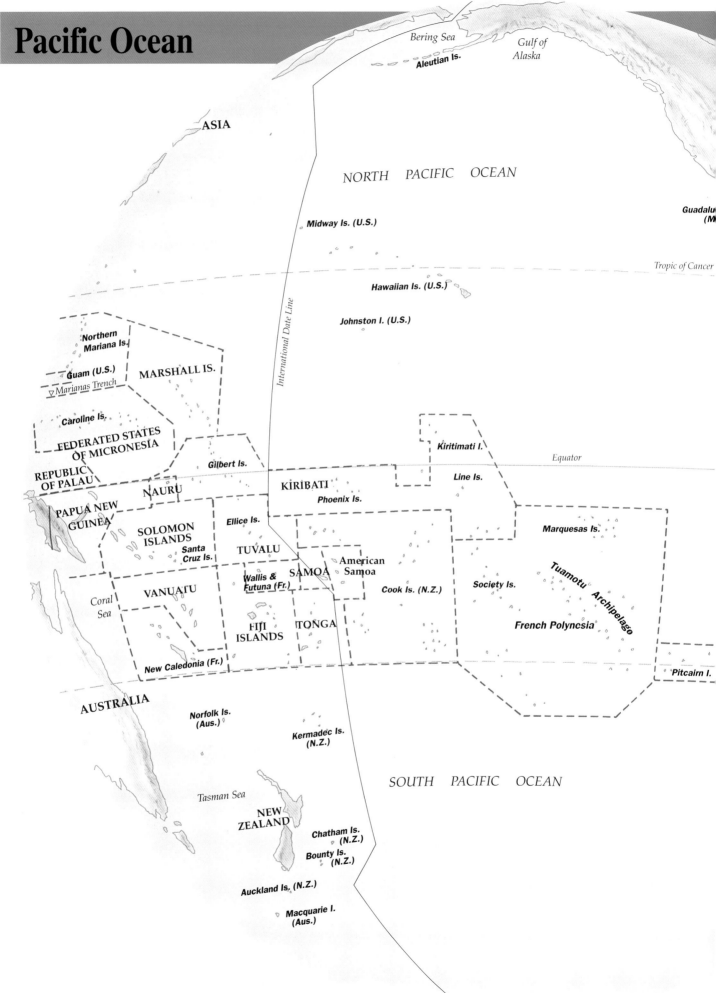

Bering Sea

Gulf of Alaska

Aleutian Is.

ASIA

NORTH   PACIFIC   OCEAN

Guadalu **(M**

Midway Is. (U.S.)

Tropic of Cancer

Hawaiian Is. (U.S.)

Johnston I. (U.S.)

Northern Mariana Is.

Guam (U.S.)

▽*Marianas Trench*

MARSHALL IS.

International Date Line

Caroline Is.

FEDERATED STATES OF MICRONESIA

Kiritimati I.

Equator

REPUBLIC OF PALAU

Gilbert Is.

NAURU

KIRIBATI

Line Is.

Phoenix Is.

PAPUA NEW GUINEA

SOLOMON ISLANDS

Ellice Is.

Marquesas Is.

Santa Cruz Is.

TUVALU

American Samoa

SAMOA

Tuamotu Archipelago

Wallis & Futuna (Fr.)

Cook Is. (N.Z.)

Society Is.

Coral Sea

VANUATU

FIJI ISLANDS

TONGA

French Polynesia

New Caledonia (Fr.)

Pitcairn I.

AUSTRALIA

Norfolk Is. (Aus.)

Kermadec Is. (N.Z.)

SOUTH   PACIFIC   OCEAN

Tasman Sea

NEW ZEALAND

Chatham Is. (N.Z.)

Bounty Is. (N.Z.)

Auckland Is. (N.Z.)

Macquarie I. (Aus.)

NORTH
AMERICA

Revilla Gigedo Is.
(Mex.)

Clipperton I.
(Fr.)

Isla del Coco
(Costa Rica)

Galápagos Is.
(Equador)

SOUTH
AMERICA

Tropic of Capricorn

Sala y Gómez (Chile)

Easter I. (Chile)

San Félix
(Chile)

Juan Fernández Is.
(Chile)

PACIFIC OCEAN

Area: 181,000,000 sq km
(69,884,500 sq miles)

Deepest point:
11,033m (33,198ft)
in the Marianas Trench

PALAU

Area: 488 sq km (188 sq miles)
Population: 20,000
Capital: Koror (pop 14,000)

FEDERATED STATES OF MICRONESIA

Area: 702 sq km (271 sq miles)
Population: 108,000
Capital: Palikir (pop 7,000)

MARSHALL ISLANDS

Area: 181 sq km (70 sq miles)
Population: 59,000
Capital: Majuro (pop 25,000)

NAURU

Area: 21 sq km (8 sq miles)
Population: 13,000
Capital: Yaren (pop 13,000)

KIRIBATI

Area: 728 sq km (281 sq miles)
Population: 103,000
Capital: Bairiki (pop 42,000)

International Date Line

The international date line runs
north-south through the central
Pacific Ocean. When crossing the
line from east to west, travellers
lose one day. When crossing from
west to east, they gain a day.

This is because there is a 24-hour
difference between the time on
either side of the line. The line does
not follow longitude 180 degrees
exactly. It bends around islands to
avoid confusion.

TUVALU

Area: 25 sq km (10 sq miles)
Population: 11,000
Capital: Fongafale (pop 6,000)

SAMOA

Area: 2,842 sq km (1,097 sq miles)
Population: 177,000
Capital: Apia (pop 40,000)

FIJI ISLANDS

Area: 18,274 sq km (7,056 sq
miles)
Population: 893,000
Capital: Suva (pop 210,000)

TONGA

Area: 699 sq km (270 sq miles)
Population: 112,000
Capital: Nuku'alofa (pop 35,000)

Atlantic Ocean

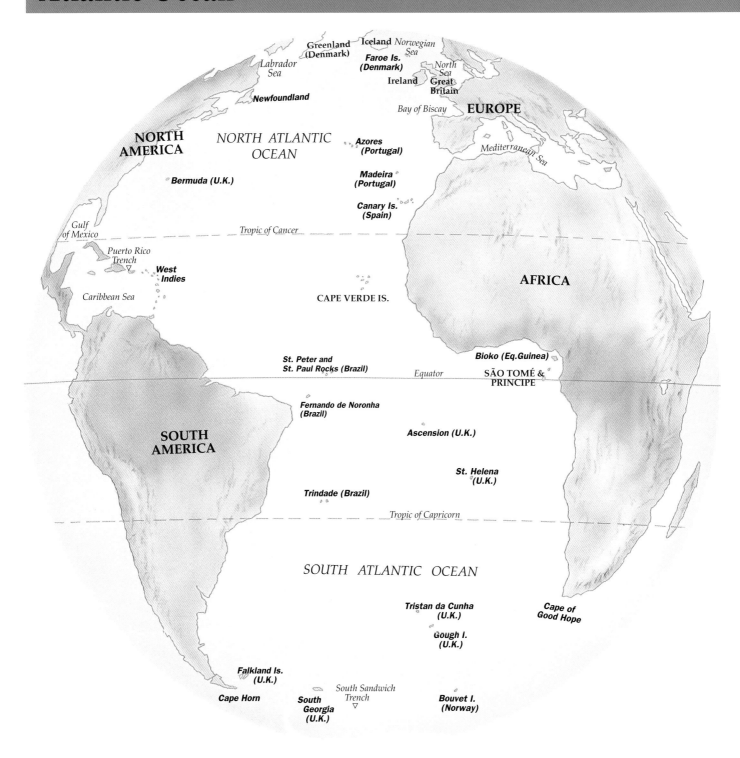

Greenland
(Denmark)
Iceland
Norwegian Sea
Faroe Is.
(Denmark)
North Sea
Ireland
Great Britain
Labrador Sea
Newfoundland
Bay of Biscay
EUROPE
NORTH AMERICA
NORTH ATLANTIC OCEAN
Azores (Portugal)
Mediterranean Sea
Bermuda (U.K.)
Madeira (Portugal)
Gulf of Mexico
Canary Is. (Spain)
Tropic of Cancer
Puerto Rico Trench
West Indies
AFRICA
Caribbean Sea
CAPE VERDE IS.
St. Peter and St. Paul Rocks (Brazil)
Bioko (Eq.Guinea)
Equator
SÃO TOMÉ & PRINCIPE
Fernando de Noronha (Brazil)
SOUTH AMERICA
Ascension (U.K.)
St. Helena (U.K.)
Trindade (Brazil)
Tropic of Capricorn
SOUTH ATLANTIC OCEAN
Tristan da Cunha (U.K.)
Cape of Good Hope
Gough I. (U.K.)
Falkland Is. (U.K.)
Cape Horn
South Sandwich Trench
South Georgia (U.K.)
Bouvet I. (Norway)

ATLANTIC OCEAN
Area: 81,500,000 sq km
(31,467,330 sq miles)
Deepest point: 9,220m (30,250ft)
in the Puerto Rico Trench

INDIAN OCEAN
Area: 74,000,000 sq km
(28,571,560 sq miles)
Deepest point: 7,450m (24,442ft)
in the Java Trench

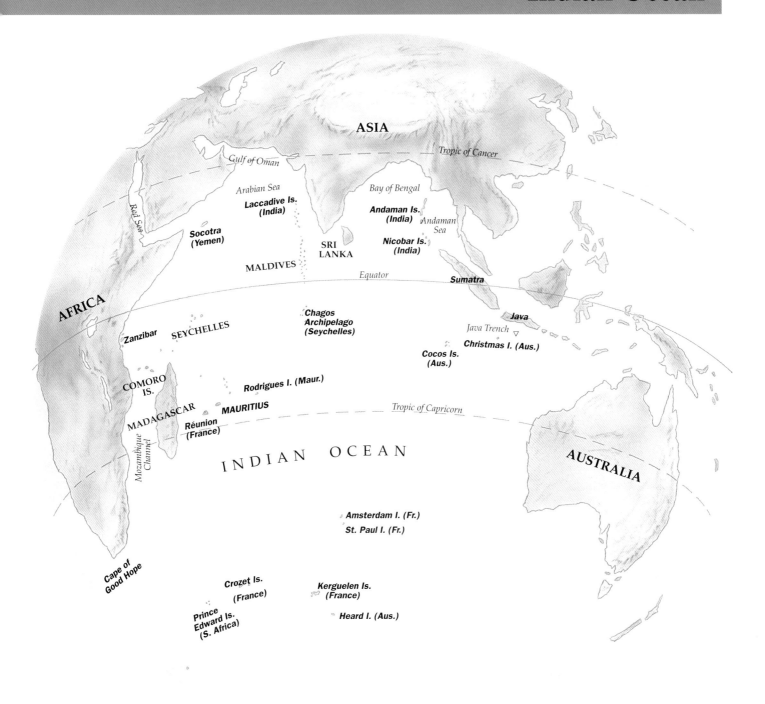

ASIA

Tropic of Cancer

Gulf of Oman

Arabian Sea

Bay of Bengal

**Laccadive Is.
(India)**

**Andaman Is.
(India)**

*Andaman
Sea*

**Socotra
(Yemen)**

SRI
LANKA

**Nicobar Is.
(India)**

Red Sea

MALDIVES

Equator

Sumatra

AFRICA

**Chagos
Archipelago
(Seychelles)**

Java

Java Trench

Zanzibar **SEYCHELLES**

Christmas I. (Aus.)

**Cocos Is.
(Aus.)**

**COMORO
IS.**

Rodrigues I. (Maur.)

Tropic of Capricorn

MADAGASCAR **MAURITIUS**

*Réunion
(France)*

I N D I A N   O C E A N

AUSTRALIA

*Mozambique
Channel*

Amsterdam I. (Fr.)

St. Paul I. (Fr.)

**Cape of
Good Hope**

**Crozet Is.
(France)**

**Kerguelen Is.
(France)**

**Prince
Edward Is.
(S. Africa)**

Heard I. (Aus.)

ANTARCTICA

MALDIVES
Area: 298 sq km (115 sq miles)
Population: 349,000
Capital: Male (pop 83,000)

SEYCHELLES
Area: 404 sq km (156 sq miles)
Population: 81,000
Capital: Victoria (pop 25,000)

MAURITIUS
Area: 1,865 sq km (720 sq miles)
Population: 1,230,000
Capital: Port Louis (pop 143,000)

Arctic Ocean

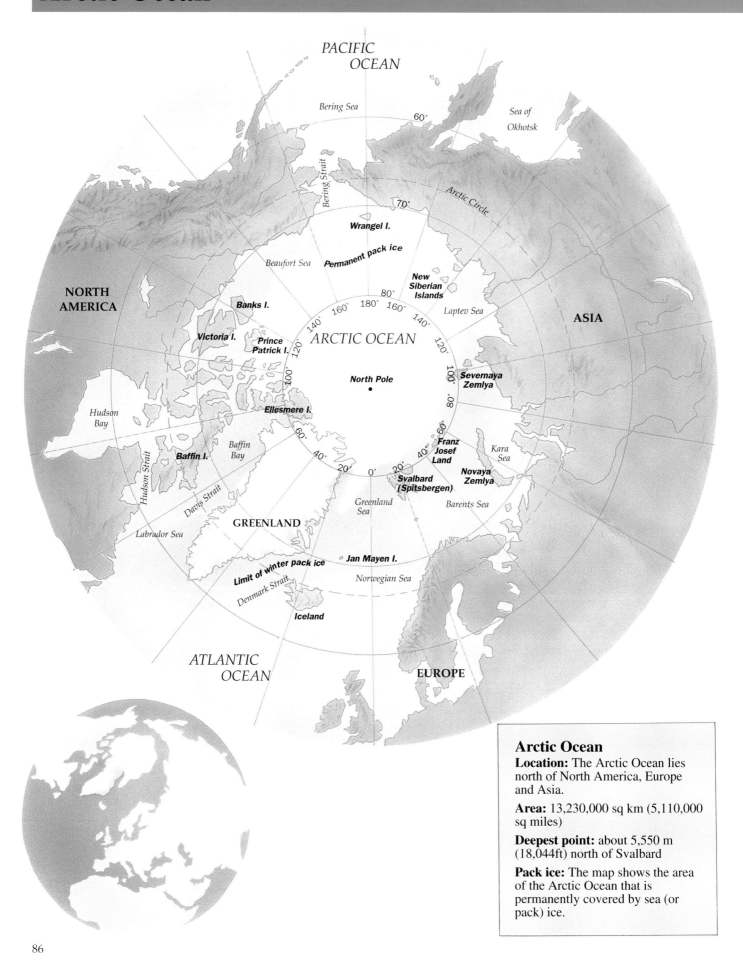

PACIFIC OCEAN

Bering Sea

Sea of Okhotsk

60°

Arctic Circle

70°

Bering Strait

Wrangel I.

Beaufort Sea

Permanent pack ice

New Siberian Islands

NORTH AMERICA

80°

Banks I.

160° 180° 160°

140° 140°

Laptev Sea

ASIA

Victoria I.

ARCTIC OCEAN

120°

120°

Prince Patrick I.

100°

Severnaya Zemlya

North Pole

100°

Hudson Bay

80°

Ellesmere I.

60°

Franz Josef Land

Kara Sea

40°

Baffin I.

Baffin Bay

60°

40°

Novaya Zemlya

Hudson Strait

20°

20°

Svalbard (Spitsbergen)

Barents Sea

Davis Strait

0°

Greenland Sea

GREENLAND

Labrador Sea

Jan Mayen I.

Norwegian Sea

Limit of winter pack ice

Denmark Strait

Iceland

ATLANTIC OCEAN

EUROPE

Arctic Ocean

Location: The Arctic Ocean lies north of North America, Europe and Asia.

Area: 13,230,000 sq km (5,110,000 sq miles)

Deepest point: about 5,550 m (18,044ft) north of Svalbard

Pack ice: The map shows the area of the Arctic Ocean that is permanently covered by sea (or pack) ice.

Antarctica

Location: Antarctica is a frozen continent at the South Pole. The waters around Antarctica are sometimes called the Southern Ocean, but many geographers still consider these waters to be part of the Pacific, Atlantic and Indian oceans.

Area: About 14,000,000 sq km (about 5,405,000 sq miles)

Population: None permanent

ATLANTIC OCEAN

South Georgia
South Sandwich Is.

60°

Antarctic Circle

Falkland Is.
South Orkney Is.

70°

Coats Land

Dronning Maud Land

Enderby Land

South Shetland Is.

Weddell Sea

80°

Heard I.

Cape Horn

SOUTH AMERICA

Antarctic Peninsula

Ronne Ice Shelf

20° 0° 20° 40°

INDIAN OCEAN

Peter I.

Vinson Massif 5140m
Ellsworth Mts

South Pole

80°

Wilhelm II Coast

Ellsworth Land

100°

Vostok Station

Amundsen Sea

Marie Byrd Land

120° 140° 160° 180° 160°

Ross Ice Shelf

Transantarctic Mts

Wilkes Land

McMurdo Station
Mt. Erebus 3794m

Victoria Land

Ross Sea

Franklin I.

Coulman I.

PACIFIC OCEAN

Limit of winter pack ice

Scott I.

Balleny Is.

Index

90

Göteborg 48 F5
Gotland 48 G5
Gough I. 84
Governador Valadares 36 E4
Grafton 80 E3
Grampian Mts. 45 E2
Granada (Nicaragua) 31 G5
Granada (Spain) 46 D4
Gran Canaria 46 I6
Gran Chaco 37 C5
Grand Bahama I. 32 B1
Grand Canyon 29 E3
Grand Coulee Dam 29 D1
Grand Forks 26 B1
Grand Island 26 B2
Grand Junction 29 F3
Grand Rapids 27 D2
Grand Turk 33 C2
Grantham 45 F4
Granville 42 C2
Graz 50 D3
Great Abaco I. 32 B1
Great Artesian Basin 80 D3
Great Australian Bight 80 B4
Great Barrier Reef 80 D2
Great Basin 29 D3
Great Bear L. 18 B2
Breat Bend 26 B3
Great Dividing Range 80 D4
Greater Antilles 32 B3
Great Exuma I. 32 B2
Great Falls 29 E1
Great Inagua I. 33 C2
Great Karroo 76 B3
Great Ouse R. 45 G4
Great Plains 29 F1
Great Rift Valley 71 F4
Great Salt Lake 29 E2
Great Sandy Desert 80 B3
Great Slave Lake 18 B2
Great Victoria Desert 80 B3
Great Wall of China 64 D2
Great Yarmouth 45 G4
Greece 53 E3
Greeley 29 G2
Green Bay 27 D2
Greenland 19 E2
Greenland Sea 86
Greenock 45 D3
Greensboro 25 G1
Greenville (Miss.) 24 D2
Greenville (S.C.) 25 F2
Grenada 33 E4
Grenoble 43 F4
Gretna Green 45 E3
Grimsby 45 F4
Groningen 50 B1
Gross Glockner 50 C3
Grozny 54 B2
Guadalajara (Mexico) 30 D3
Guadalajara (Spain) 47 D2
Guadalcanal I. 81 F1
Guadalupe I. 82
Guadalupe Peak 24 B2
Guadeloupe 33 E3
Guadiana R. 46 C3
Guam 82
Guanabacoa 32 A2
Guane 32 A2
Guangzhou 65 D3
Guantánamo 32 B2
Guasave 30 C2
Guatemala 31 F4
Guatemala City 31 F5
Guaviare R. 36 C2
Guayaquil 36 B3
Guernsey 45 H5
Guiana Highlands 36 C2
Guildford 45 F5
Guilin 64 D3

Guinea 72 D4
Guinea-Bissau 72 D4
Güines 32 A2
Guiyang 64 C3
Gujranwala 63 C2
Gulf, The 60 D3
Gulfport 25 E2
Gulu 75 C1
Gunnbjorn, Mt 19 F2
Guntur 63 E5
Gusau 73 H4
Guwahati 63 G3
Guyana 36 D2
Gwadar 62 A3
Gwalior 63 D3
Gweru 76 B2
Gyandzha 54 B2
Györ 50 D3

H
Haarlem 50 A1
Hadejia R. 73 I4
Hadhramaut 60 C5
Hafar 60 C3
Hafnarfjördhur 48 A2
Hagerstown 23 E4
Hague, The 50 A1
Haifa 59 C3
Haikou 64 D4
Hail 60 B3
Hainan 64 D4
Haiphong 66 B1
Haiti 33 C2
Hakodate 65 F2
Halberstadt 50 C2
Halifax (Canada) 19 D3
Halifax (U.K.) 45 F4
Halle 50 C2
Halmahera 67 D3
Halmstad 48 F5
Hama 59 D3
Hamadan 60 C2
Hamar 48 E4
Hamburg 50 C1
Hämeenlinna 48 I4
Hamhung 65 E2
Hamilton (Canada) 19 D3
Hamilton (New Zealand) 81 G4
Hamilton (U.) 27 E3
Hamilton (U.K.) 45 D3
Hammerfest 48 H1
Hampton 23 F5
Handan 65 D2
Hangzhou 65 E3
Hanoi 66 B1
Hanover 50 B1
Haradh 60 C4
Harar 71 G4
Harare 76 C2
Harbin 65 E1
Hardanger Plateau 48 D4
Hargeisa 71 G4
Härnösand 48 G3
Harrisburg 23 F3
Harrison 24 D1
Harrisonburg 23 E4
Harrogate 45 F4
Harstad 48 G2
Hartford 23 G3
Hartlepool 45 F3
Harz Mts. 50 C2
Hasselt 43 F1
Hastings (Nebr.) 26 B2
Hastings (New Zealand) 81 G4
Hastings (U.K.) 45 G5
Hat Yai 66 B3
Hatteras, Cape 25 G1
Hattiesburg 25 E2
Haugesund 48 D4
Havana 32 A2
Havre 29 F1
Hawaii 28 A1

Hawaiian Is. 82
Hawick 45 E3
Hays 26 B3
Heard I. 85
Hebron 59 C4
Hefei 65 D3
Heidelberg 50 B2
Heilbronn 50 B2
Heimaey I. 48 A2
Hejaz 60 A4
Helena 29 E1
Helsingborg 48 F5
Helsinki 48 I4
Hengyang 65 D3
Herat 62 A2
Hereford 45 E4
Hermosillo 30 B2
Herning 48 E5
Hidalgo del Parral 30 C2
Hierro 46 I6
High Atlas Mts. 70 B1
High Point 25 G1
Hilo 28 A1
Himalayas 63 D2, 64 B3
Hindu Kush 62 B2
Hinggan Range, Greater 65 D1
Hinggan Range, Lesser 65 E1
Hiroshima 65 F2
Ho 73 G5
Hobart 80 D5
Hódmezővásárhely 51 E3
Hofn 48 C2
Hohhot 65 D2
Hokkaido 65 F2
Holguin 32 B2
Holon 59 C3
Holstebro 48 E5
Holyhead 45 D4
Holy I. 45 F3
Homs 59 D3
Honduras 31 G5
Honduras, Gulf of 31 G4
Hong Kong 65 D3
Honiara 81 E1
Honolulu 28 A1
Honshu 65 F2
Hoover Dam 29 E3
Hopkinsville 22 B5
Hormuz, Strait of 61 E3
Hospitalet 47 G2
Hot Springs 24 D2
Houston 24 C3
Hovsgol L. 64 C1
Howrah 63 F4
Hradec Králové 50 D2
Huainan 65 D2
Huambo 74 B3
Huancayo 36 B4
Huang He R. 64 C2
Huangshi 65 D3
Huascaran, Mt. 36 B3
Hubli 63 D5
Huddersfield 45 F4
Hudson Bay 19 C3
Hudson R. 23 G3
Hudson Strait 19 D2
Hue 66 B2
Huelva 46 B4
Huesca 47 E1
Hull 19 D3
Humber R. 45 F4
Humboldt R. 28 D2
Hungary 51 E3
Huntington 22 D4
Huntsville 25 E2
Huron 26 B2
Huron L. 19 C3
Hutchinson 26 B3
Hvannadalshnükur, Mt. 48 B2
Hyderabad (India) 63 D5
Hyderabad (Pakistan) 62 B3

I
Iaşi 53 F1
Ibadan 73 G5
Ibagué 36 B2
Ibiza 47 F3
Ica 36 B4
Iceland 48 A2
Idaho 29 E2
Idaho Falls 29 E2
Ife 73 G5
IJsselmeer 50 A1
Ikaria 53 F4
Ilebo 74 B2
Ilesha 73 G5
Ilhéus 36 F4
Iligan 67 D3
Illinois 27 D3
Illinois R. 27 C2
Iloilo 67 D2
Ilorin 73 G5
Imphal 63 G4
Inari, L. 49 I2
Inchon 65 E2
Independence 26 C3
India 63 D4
Indiana 27 D2
Indianapolis 27 D3
Indian Ocean 85
Indigirka R. 55 G1
Indonesia 67 C4
Indore 63 D4
Indus R. 62 B3
Inhambane 76 C2
Inn R. 50 C2
Inner Hebrides 45 C2
Innsbruck 50 C3
Inowroclaw 50 E1
International Date Line 82
International Falls 26 C1
Invercargill 81 F5
Inverness 45 D2
Ioannina 53 D3
Iona 45 C2
Ionian Sea 53 D3
Iowa 26 C2
Iowa City 27 C2
Ipoh 66 B3
Ipswich (Australia) 80 E3
Ipswich (U.K.) 45 G4
Iquique 36 B4
Iquitos 36 B3
Iran 61 D2
Irapuato 30 D3
Iraq 60 B2
Irbid 59 C3
Irbil 60 B1
Ireland, Republic of 44 C4
Irian Jaya 67 E4
Iringa 75 D2
Irish Sea 45 D4
Irkutsk 55 E2
Ironwood 27 C1
Irrawaddy R. 66 A2
Irtysh R. 54 C2
Irún 47 E1
Isafjördhur 48 A1
Ischia 52 B3
Isère R. 43 F4
Iskenderun 59 D2
Islamabad 63 C2
Islay 45 C3
Ismoili Somoni Peak 54 C3
Isparta 58 B2
Israel 59 C3
Istanbul 58 B1
Italy 52 B2
Ithaca 23 F3
Ivanovo 54 B2
Iwo 73 G5

Izhevsk 54 B2
Izmir 58 A2
Izmit 58 B1

J
Jabalpur 63 D4
Jackson (Miss.) 24 D2
Jackson (Tenn.) 25 E1
Jacksonville (Fla.) 25 F2
Jacksonville (N.C.) 25 G2
Jacmel 33 C3
Jaén 46 D4
Jaffna 63 E7
Jaipur 63 D3
Jakarta 66 B4
Jalalabad 62 C2
Jalapa Enriquez 30 E4
Jamaica 32 B3
Jambi 66 B4
James Baý 19 C3
James R. (S. Dak.) 26 B2
James R. (Va.) 23 E4
Jamestown (N. Dak.) 26 B1
Jamestown (N.Y.) 22 E3
Jammu 63 C2
Jamnagar 62 B4
Jamshedpur 63 F4
Janesville 27 D2
Jan Mayen I. 86
Japan 65 F2
Japan, Sea of 65 F2
Japurá R. 36 B3
Jardines de la Reina 32 B2
Jaroslaw 51 F2
Java 66 B4
Java Sea 67 C4
Java Trench 85
Jebel Marra, Mt. 71 E3
Jefferson City 26 C3
Jérémie 32 C3
Jerez de la Frontera 46 B4
Jersey 45 H5
Jersey City 23 G3
Jerusalem 59 C4
Jhansi 63 D3
Jiddah 60 A4
Jilava 50 D2
Jilin 65 E2
Jinan 65 D2
Jingdezhen 65 D3
Jinja 75 C1
Jinzhou 65 E2
Jixi 65 E1
Jizan 60 B5
João Pessoa 36 F3
Jodhpur 63 C3
Joensuu 49 J3
Johannesburg 76 B3
John Day River 28 C1
John o'Groats 45 E1
Johnson City 25 F1
Johnston I. 82
Johnstown 22 E3
Johor Baharu 66 B3
Jonesboro 24 D1
Jönköping 48 F5
Joplin 26 C3
Jordan 59 D4
Jordan R. 59 C3
Jos Plateau 73 H4
Jostedal Glacier 48 D4
Juan Fernández Is. 37 B6
Juba 71 F4
Juiz de Fora 37 E5
Jullundur 63 D2
Junction City 26 B3
Juneau 28 B1
Jura 45 D3
Jura Mts. 43 G3
Juruá R. 36 C3
Jutland 48 E5

Jyväskylä 49 I3

K
K2 Mt. 62 D1
Kabalo 74 C2
Kabul 62 B2
Kabwe 76 B1
Kaduna 73 H4
Kafue R. 76 B2
Kagoshima 65 E3
Kahoolawe 28 A1
Kaifeng 65 D2
Kainji L. 73 G4
Kajaani 49 I3
Kalahari Desert 76 B2
Kalamata 53 E4
Kalamazoo 27 D2
Kalat 62 B3
Kalémié 74 C2
Kalgoorlie 80 B4
Kalimantan 67 C4
Kaliningrad 54 A2
Kalispell 29 E1
Kalisz 50 E2
Kallavesi L. 49 I3
Kalmar 48 G5
Kamchatka Peninsula 55 G2
Kamina 74 B2
Kampala 75 C1
Kananga 74 B2
Kanazawa 65 F2
Kandahar 62 B2
Kandy 63 E7
Kangaroo I. 80 C4
Kankakee 27 D2
Kankan 72 E4
Kannapolis 25 F1
Kano 73 H4
Kanpur 63 E3
Kansas 26 B3
Kansas City (Kans.) 26 C3
Kansas City (Mo.) 26 C3
Kansas R. 26 B3
Kaolack 72 C4
Karachi 62 B4
Karakoram Range 63 D1
Karaman 59 C2
Kara Sea 55 C1
Karbala 60 B2
Kariba Dam 76 B2
Kariba L. 76 B2
Karlskrona 48 F5
Karlsruhe 50 B2
Karlstad 48 F4
Karpathos 53 F4
Kars 59 E1
Kasai R. 74 B2
Kasama 75 C2
Kashan 60 C2
Kashi 64 A2
Kassala 71 F3
Kassel 50 B2
Katahdin, Mt. 23 I1
Katmandu 63 F3
Katowice 51 E2
Katsina 73 H4
Kattegat 48 E5
Kauai 28 A1
Kavalla 53 E3
Kawasaki 65 F2
Kayes 70 A3
Kayseri 59 C2
Kazakhstan 54 C2
Kazan 54 B2
Kebnekaise, Mt. 48 G2
Kecskemét 51 E3
Keetmanshoop 76 A3
Kefallinia 53 D3
Keflavik 48 A2

St. Petersburg (Fa.) 25 F3
St. Petersburg (Russia) 54 A2
St. Pierre & Miquelon 19 E3
St. Pölten 50 D2
St-Quentin 42 E2
St. Tropez 43 G5
St Vincent & The Grenadines 33 E4
Sakai 65 F2
Sakakawea L. 26 A1
Sakarya R. 58 B1
Sakhalin I. 55 G2
Sala y Gómez 83
Sal I. 72 B1
Salalah 61 D5
Salamanca 46 C2
Salekhard 54 C1
Salem (India) 63 D6
Salem (Ore.) 28 C2
Salerno 52 C3
Salina 26 B3
Salisbury (Md.) 23 F4
Salisbury (U.K.) 45 F5
Salta 37 C5
Saltillo 30 D2
Salt Lake City 29 E2
Salto 37 D6
Salton Sea 29 D4
Salvador 36 F4
Salween R. 64 C3
Salzburg 50 C3
Salzgitter 50 C1
Samar 67 D2
Samara 54 B2
Samarinda 67 C4
Samarqand 54 C3
Samoa 82
Samos 53 F4
Samothraki 53 E3
Sam Rayburn Res. 24 D2
Samsun 59 D1
San R. 51 F2
Sana 60 B5
San Ambrosio I. 37 B5
San Angelo 24 B2
San Antonio 24 C3
San Bernardino 28 D4
San Carlos 67 D2
Sancti Spiritus 32 B2
San Cristóbal 36 B2
San Diego 28 D4
Sandviken 48 G4
San Félix I. 37 A5
San Fernando 46 B4
San Francisco 28 C3
Sangihe Is. 67 D3
San Joaquin R. 28 C3
San Jose 28 C3
San José 31 H6
San Juan (Argentina) 37 C6
San Juan (Puerto Rico) 33 D3
Sanlúcar 46 B4
San Luis Potosi 30 D3
San Marino 52 B2
San Miguel 31 G5
San Miguel de Tucumán 37 C5
San Pedro Sula 31 G4
San Salvador 31 G5
San Salvador I. 32 C2
San Sebastián 47 E1
Santa Ana (Calif.) 28 D4
Santa Ana (El Salvador) 31 G5
Santa Antão 72 A1
Santa Barbara 28 D4
Santa Clara 32 B2
Santa Cruz (Bolivia) 36 C4
Santa Cruz (Canary Is.) 46 I5
Santa Cruz Is. 82
Santa Fe (Argentina) 37 C6
Santa Fe (N. Mex.) 29 F3
Santa Maria (Brazil) 37 D5
Santa Maria (Calif.) 28 C4
Santa Marta 36 B1

Santander 46 D1
Santa Rosa 28 C3
Santee R. 25 F2
Santiago (Chile) 37 B6
Santiago (Dominican Republic) 33 C3
Santiago de Compostela 46 A1
Santiago de Cuba 32 B2
Santiago del Estero 37 C5
Santiago Mts. 24 B3
Santo Domingo 33 D3
Santos 37 E5
Sao Francisco R. E4
São Luis 36 E3
Saône R. 43 F3
São Paulo 37 E5
São Tiago I. 72 B1
São Tomé 74 A1
Sao Tomé & Principe 74 A1
Sapele 73 H5
Sapporo 65 F2
Sarajevo 53 D2
Sarasota 25 F2
Saratov 54 B2
Sarawak 67 C3
Sardinia 52 A3
Sargodha 63 C2
Sarh 71 D4
Sark 45 H5
Sarmi 67 E4
Saskatchewan 18 B3
Saskatchewan R. 18 E3
Saskatoon 18 B3
Sassandra R. 72 E5
Sassari 52 A3
Satu Mare 53 E1
Saudi Arabia 60 B4
Sault Ste. Marie (Canada) 19 C3
Sault Ste. Marie (Mich.) 27 E1
Sava R. 52 C2
Savannah 25 F2
Savannah R. 25 F2
Sayan Mts. 55 D2
Scafell Pike 45 E3
Scarborough (Tobago) 33 E4
Scarborough (U.K.) 45 F3
Schaffhausen 43 H3
Schweinfurt 50 C2
Schwerin 50 C1
Scilly, Isles of 45 C6
Scotland 45 D2
Scott I. 87
Scottsbluff 26 A2
Scranton 23 F3
Scunthorpe 45 F4
Scutari L. 53 D2
Seattle 28 C1
Ségou 70 B3
Segovia 46 C2
Seine R. 42 D2
Sekondi-Takoradi 73 F5
Selma 25 E2
Selvas 36 C3
Semarang 67 C4
Semipalatinsk 55 D2
Sendai 65 F2
Senegal 72 D4
Senegal R. 72 D3
Seoul 65 E2
Sepik River 80 D1
Serbia 53 D2
Serowe 76 B2
Serra da Estrela 46 B2
Serra de Alvelos 46 B3
Serrai 53 E3
Serrania de Cuenca 47 E2
Sète 42 E5
Sétif 70 C1
Setúbal 46 A3
Sevastopol 54 A2
Severnaya Zemlya 55 E1
Severn R. 45 E5

Seville 46 C4
Seward 28 B1
Seychelles 85
Seydhisfjordhur 48 C2
Seyhan R. 59 C2
Sfax 70 D1
Shache 64 A2
Shanghai 65 E3
Shannon R. 44 B4
Shantou 65 D3
Shaoguan 65 D3
Shaoyang 64 D3
Sharjah 61 E3
Shebelle R. 71 G4
Sheboygan 27 D2
Sheffield 45 F4
Shenandoah R. 23 E4
Shenyang 65 E2
Sherbro I. 72 D5
Sheridan 29 F2
Sherman 24 C2
Shetland Is. 45 H2
Shijiazhuang 65 D2
Shikoku 65 F2
Shiraz 60 D3
Shire R. 76 C2
Shkodër 53 D2
Sholapur 63 D5
Shreveport 24 D2
Shrewsbury 45 E4
Shumen 53 F2
Shuqra 60 C6
Shushtar 60 C2
Siberut 66 A4
Sibiu 53 E2
Sicily 52 B4
Sidi-bel-Abbès 70 B1
Sidon 59 C2
Siedlce 51 F1
Siena 52 B2
Sierra de Gredos 46 C2
Sierra Leone 72 D5
Sierra Madre del Sur 30 E4
Sierra Madre Occidental 30 C2
Sierra Madre Oriental 30 E3
Sierra Morena 46 C3
Sierra Nevada (Spain) 46 D4
Sierra Nevada (USA) 28 D3
Siglufjödhur 48 B1
Sil R. 46 B1
Silgarhi 63 E3
Silifke 59 C2
Silistra 53 F2
Simeulue 66 A3
Simpson Desert 80 C3
Singapore 66 B3
Sintang 67 C3
Sinuiju 65 E2
Sioux City 26 B2
Sioux Falls 26 B2
Siping 65 E2
Siracusa 52 C4
Siret R. 53 F2
Sisophon 66 B2
Sitka 28 B1
Sivas 59 D2
Skagerrak 48 E5
Skagway 28 B1
Skegness 45 G4
Skellefteå 48 H3
Skellefte R. 48 G3
Skien 48 E4
Skiros 53 E3
Skopje 53 D3
Skye 45 C2
Slagelse 48 E5
Slavonski Brod 53 D2
Sligo 44 B3
Sliven 53 F2
Slovakia 51 E2
Slovenia 52 C1

Slupsk 50 D1
Smederevo 53 D2
Smolensk 54 A2
Snake R. 29 D1
Snowdon, Mt. 45 D4
Society Is. 82
Socotra 85
Sofia 53 E2
Sogne Fiord 48 D4
Sokodé 73 G5
Sokoto 73 H4
Sokoto R. 73 G4
Solomon Is. 81 F1
Solomon Sea 80 E1
Solothurn 43 G3
Somalia 71 G4
Somerset I. 19 C2
Somesul R. 53 E1
Somme R. 42 E2
Songkhla 66 B3
Soria 47 D2
Sorocaba 37 E5
Sousse 70 D1
Southampton 45 F5
Southampton I. 19 C2
South Australia 80 C3
South Bend 27 D2
South Carolina 25 F2
South China Sea 67 C2
South Dakota 26 A1
South Downs 45 F5
Southend-on-Sea 45 G5
Southern Alps 81 F5
Southern Uplands 45 D3
South Georgia 84
South I. 81 F5
South Korea 65 E2
South Orkney Is. 87
South Pole 87
Southport 45 E4
South Sandwich Is. 87
South Sandwich Trench 84
South Shetland Is. 87
South Shields 45 F3
South Uist 44 C2
Spain 46 C3
Spanish Town 32 B3
Sparks 28 D3
Spartanburg 25 F2
Spencer 26 B2
Spey R. 45 E2
Split 52 C2
Spokane 29 D1
Springfield (Ill.) 27 D3
Springfield (Mass.) 23 G3
Springfield (Mo.) 26 C3
Springfield (O.) 27 E3
Springfield (Vt.) 23 H2
Springs 76 B3
Sri Lanka 63 E7
Srinagar 63 C2
Stafford 45 E4
Stamford 23 G3
Stanley 37 D8
Stanovoy Range 55 F2
Stara Zagora 53 E2
State College 23 E3
Stavanger 48 D4
Steinkjer 48 E3
Sterling 29 G2
Steubenville 27 E2
Stewart I. 81 F5
Steyr 50 D2
Stockholm 48 G4
Stockport 45 E4
Stockton (Calif.) 28 C3
Stockton (England) 45 F3
Stoke-on-Trent 45 E4
Stornoway 45 C1
Stralsund 50 C1

Stranraer 45 D3
Strasbourg 43 G2
Struma R. 53 E3
Stuttgart 50 B2
Subotica 53 D1
Sucre 36 C4
Sudan 71 E3
Sudbury 19 C3
Sudeten Mts. 50 D2
Suez 71 F2
Suez Canal 71 F1
Sukabumi 66 B4
Sukkur 62 B3
Sula Is. 67 D4
Sulaiman Range 62 B3
Sulawesi 67 D4
Sulu Sea 67 C3
Sumatra 66 B3
Sumba 67 C4
Sumbawa 67 C4
Sumter 25 F2
Sunbury 23 F3
Sunderland 45 F3
Sundsvall 48 G3
Superior 26 C1
Superior, L. 19 C3
Surabaya 67 C4
Surakarta 67 C4
Surat 63 C4
Surgut 54 C1
Surinam 36 D2
Surtsey I. 48 A2
Susquehanna R. 23 F3
Suzhou 65 E3
Svalbard (Spitsbergen) 86
Sverdlovsk, see Yekaterinburg
Swansea 45 E5
Swaziland 76 C3
Sweden 48 F4
Swindon 45 F5
Switzerland 43 G3
Sydney (Australia) 80 E4
Sydney (Canada) 19 D3
Syracuse 23 F2
Syr Darya R. 54 C2
Syria 59 D3
Syrian Desert 59 D3
Szczecin 50 D1
Szeged 51 E3
Székesfehérvár 50 E3
Szombathely 50 D3

T
Tabora 75 C2
Tabriz 60 C1
Tabuk 60 A3
Tacna 36 B4
Tacoma 28 C1
Taegu 65 E2
Taejon 65 E2
Tahat, Mt. 70 C2
Tahoe L. 28 D3
Taichung 65 E3
Tainan 65 E3
Taipei 65 E3
Taiwan 65 E3
Taiyuan 65 D2
Taiz 60 B6
Tajikistan 54 C3
Tajo (Tagus) R. 46 C3
Taklimakan Desert 64 A2
Talaud Is. 67 D3
Talavera 46 C3
Talca 37 B6
Talcahuano 37 B6
Tallahassee 25 F2
Tallinn 54 A2
Tambov 54 B2
Tampa 25 F3
Tampere 48 H4
Tampico 30 E3

Tana L. 71 F3
Tana R. 75 D2
Tandil 37 D6
Tanga 75 D2
Tanganyika L. 75 C2
Tangier 70 B1
Tangshan 65 D2
Tanimbar Is. 67 E4
Tanjungkarang 66 B4
Tanzania 75 C2
Tapachula 31 F5
Tapajós R. 36 D3
Taranto 52 C3
Tarbes 42 D5
Tarkwa 73 F5
Tarragona 47 F2
Tarsus 59 C2
Tashkent (see Toshkent)
Tasmania 80 D5
Tasman Sea 81 F4
Taunton 45 E5
Taupo L. 81 G4
Taurus Mts. 59 C2
Tawau 67 C3
Tay R. 45 E2
Tbilisi 54 B2
Tegucigalpa 31 G5
Tehran 60 D1
Teide, Pico de 46 I5
Tekirdag 58 A1
Tel Aviv-Yafo 59 C3
Temuco 37 B6
Tenby 45 D5
Tenerife 46 I5
Tennant Creek 80 C2
Tennessee 25 E1
Tennessee R. 25 E2
Tepic 30 D3
Teresina 36 E3
Terni 52 B2
Terre Haute 27 D3
Tete 76 C2
Tétouan 70 B1
Texarkana 24 D2
Texas 24 C2
Texoma L. 24 C2
Thabana Ntlenyana 76 B3
Thailand 66 B2
Thailand, Gulf of 66 B2
Thames R. 45 F5
Thar Desert 62 C3
Thasos 53 E3
Thessaloniki 53 E3
Thief River Falls 26 B1
Thiès 72 C4
Thika 75 D2
Thimphu 63 F3
Thionville 43 G2
Thira 53 E4
Three Gorges Dam 64 D3
Thule 19 D2
Thun 43 G3
Thunder Bay 19 C3
Thuringian Forest 50 C2
Thurso 45 E1
Tianjin 65 D2
Tian Shan 64 A2
Tiber R. 52 B2
Tiberias L. 59 C3
Tibesti Mts. 71 D2
Tibetan Plateau 64 B2
Ticino R. 52 A2
Tierra del Fuego 37 C8
Tigris R. 60 B2
Tijuana 30 A1
Timaru 81 G5
Timbuktu 70 B3
Timişoara 53 D2
Timmins 19 C3
Timor 67 D4
Timor Sea 80 B2
Tinos 53 E4